# Uncommon
# Martyrs

*By Fred A. Wilcox*

*Grass Roots: An Anti-Nuke Source Book*
*Waiting for an Army to Die: The Tragedy of Agent Orange*

# Uncommon Martyrs

*The Berrigans,
the Catholic Left,
and the
Plowshares Movement*

Fred A. Wilcox

Addison-Wesley Publishing Company, Inc.

*Reading, Massachusetts   Menlo Park, California*
*New York   Don Mills, Ontario*
*Wokingham, England   Amsterdam   Bonn*
*Sydney   Singapore   Tokyo   Madrid   San Juan*
*Paris   Seoul   Milan   Mexico City   Taipei*

**Library of Congress Cataloging-in-Publication Data**

Wilcox, Fred.
    Uncommon martyrs : the Berrigans, the Catholic Left, and the Plowshares movement / by Fred A. Wilcox.
       p.    cm.
    Includes bibliographical references and index.
    ISBN 0-201-52231-4
    1. Nuclear disarmament.   2. Antinuclear movement—United States. 3. Plowshares Eight (Group)  I. Title.
JX1974.7.W515  1991
327.1'74—dc20                                      90-47406
                                                        CIP

Cover design by Mike Fender
Text design by Barbara Werden
Set in 10 1/2-point Meridien by Compset, Inc., Beverly, MA

1 2 3 4 5 6 7 8 9-MW-9594939291
First printing, March 1991

. . . and they shall beat their swords into plowshares,
and their spears into pruning hooks; nation shall
not lift up sword against nation,
neither shall they learn war anymore.

ISAIAH 2:4

In my humble opinion, non-cooperation with evil is as
much a duty as is cooperation with good.

MAHATMA GANDHI

# *Acknowledgments*

I wish to thank all of the people who have so generously contributed their time and resources to this book. I particularly wish to thank Peter DeMott and the entire Grady family for their encouragement, and for offering any and all assistance for which I asked. A special thanks to Philip and Daniel Berrigan, Lin Romano, Greg Boertje, Holly and Andy Gump, and many others for their patient advice. My agent, Glen Hartley, deserves a special word of thanks, as well as my editor at Addison-Wesley, Martha Moutray. Their perceptive advice is greatly appreciated. Finally, I wish to thank all of the people, in this country and abroad, who have risked their reputations, their careers, their freedom, and their lives to work for peace. Their courage and commitment are an inspiration.

This book is dedicated with love and affection to my parents, in appreciation for teaching their children how to care.

# Contents

# Introduction

There awoke in us a feeling of living in a
house once beautiful and clean but in whose
cellars behind closed doors frightful, evil, and
fearsome things were happening. And as
doubt had slowly taken hold of us, so now
there grew within us a horror and a fear, the
first germ of abounded uncertainty.

FROM THE WHITE ROSE OPPONENTS OF
ADOLPH HITLER

At dawn on September 9, 1980, six men and two women walked across a nearly empty parking lot, climbed a short set of stairs, and quickly entered General Electric's plant at King of Prussia, Pennsylvania. For more than a year they had met to talk about this action, praying on some occasions, debating on others, sharing and sometimes laughing at their fears. All of the eight had spent time in jail or prison for their opposition to war, and knew that the consequence of this action could be years in a federal penitentiary. Inside the plant a security guard ordered them to stop, but they ignored his command, racing—as though they had memorized or instinctively knew the plant's floorplan—toward the room where nose cones for the Mark 12A warhead are tested. Once inside, they pounded on the nose cones with hammers, ripped blueprints to shreds, and poured vials of their own blood over the nose cones and prints. Sirens rang, people shouted and cursed, and the eight prayed and chanted as they were led away from the scene of their crime. The police shoved them into vans which sped toward Montgomery County jail. The action had lasted only a few moments.

Inside their cells they waited and were not fed. At noon they were taken back to the GE plant to be identified by employees. Some of the eight walked into the room, others resisted and were carried by police or security guards. The room was sepulchral and silent, with bloodstained papers marked *Top Secret* scattered about like shotgunned ducks. A gauntlet of stares, bitter, accusing, betrayed, condemning. And suddenly another order. Back to the van, to jail to wait out the afternoon. There would be no high tea, not even bread and water.

More hours passed, until, one by one they were taken from their cells, ordered to remove their shoes and pants, then led to yet another corner of the jail to wait. Bail was set at $250,000 per defendant, except for Daniel and Philip Berrigan who were held without bail. They could not—but more importantly, said the eight, *would not*—pay the bondsman. To post bail, they explained, would be to admit guilt. To cooperate would be to concede that their action was somehow illegal. This, they insisted, was simply not the case. Moreover, their intention at King of Prussia had not been simply to break the law, but to:

> . . . beat swords into plowshares . . . expose the criminality of nuclear weaponry and corporate piracy . . . We committed civil disobedience at General Electric because this genocidal entity is the fifth-leading producer of weaponry in the U.S. To maintain this position, GE

drains $3 million a day from the public treasury, an enormous larceny against the poor.

We wish also to challenge the lethal lie spun by GE through its motto, *"We bring good things to life."* As manufacturers of the Mark 12A reentry vehicle, GE actually prepares to bring good things to death. Through the Mark 12A, the threat of first-strike nuclear war grows more imminent. Thus GE advances the possible destruction of millions of innocent lives.[1]

Like most newspaper readers, I read brief accounts of the Plowshare Eight's actions. Read and reread, feeling more than a little bewildered and confused. Swords into plowshares? The symbolic pouring of human blood on nuclear warheads? Embracing jurors who found them guilty, then thanking the judge who had just ordered them to spend years in prison? Who were these people, and what on earth were they trying to accomplish? I was familiar with Daniel and Philip Berrigan, whose opposition to the Vietnam War had inspired hundreds of thousands of people in this country and abroad. Dan was a poet, a member of the Jesuit order of Catholic priests, author of forty books, and recipient of several prestigious literary awards. Philip was a published author and combat veteran of World War II. In 1974, he'd been excommunicated from the Catholic church for marrying peace activist and Catholic sister Elizabeth McAlister. Both men had spent years in prison for their beliefs, and had been nominated six times for the Nobel peace prize. About the other members of the Plowshare Eight, I knew little or nothing.

While I could not fully understand their actions, on some

level I had to admire the eight defendants for their courage, especially for their willingness to take the consequences for breaking the law. Yet conversations with friends did little to explain the meaning behind the King of Prussia action, and subsequent Plowshare actions. Indeed, said a member of the local nuclear freeze campaign's steering committee who claimed to have known the Berrigans in the 'sixties, Plowshare actions were "divisive" and "counterproductive." Another acquaintance, who spent much of his spare time collecting signatures on petitions to freeze the arms race, said, "It is so much easier to jump fences than do the nitty-gritty, grass-roots work required to stop nuclear power and end the arms race." "Nostalgia for the 'sixties, that's what this Plowshare stuff sounds like to me," said still another friend.

Driving home one evening from a meeting at which similar remarks had been made, I felt bewildered. Why did the Berrigans and their friends seem to irritate, indeed anger and frighten so many people? No one with whom I spoke had called or written the Berrigans, visited them in jail, or invited them to speak to our meetings. We had not shown Emil De Antonio's brilliant film about the King of Prussia trial, or tried to understand the religious basis for Plowshare actions. The consensus seemed to be that, while we might admire the Berrigans' courage, we must keep our distance from them personally; while we could surely respect their goals, because they were our goals as well, we should not endorse their actions.

What seemed odd then, and appears even more peculiar now, is how very easy it was to praise the courage of the Soviet Union's Andrei Sakharov while dismissing the Berrigans and friends as irresponsible anarchists. How natural to support the struggle of Poland's Solidarity movement and cheer Lech Walesa when he accepts the Nobel prize, while sending Plowshare activists to prison. How ordinary for elected officials to offer Czechoslovakia's president Vaclav Havel the key to New York City, while refusing to open a dialogue with our own religious and political dissidents.

At the trials of the Berrigans *et al.*, prosecutors insist that people who pour blood on airplanes or beat on nuclear warheads with hammers are a danger to a free society. Later, after judges sentence the protesters to longer prison terms than many first-offense rapists, drug dealers, or killers, local newspapers might describe what the defendants were wearing or how they reacted when the judge imposed the sentence. Yet always we are left wondering about these strange people, who sing as they are being taken away by federal marshals, show no bitterness toward the judge, and even thank the jurors who've convicted them. Are they hair-shirt exhibitionists and pontificating grandstanders? Or perhaps they are prophets in the truest sense, trying to warn us that, even if atomic weapons are never used against our enemies, the arms race and militarism are sacking the national treasury; destroying the infrastructure of our cities; contributing to the cancer epidemic by poisoning our environment with plutonium and radiation; and draining money that might be used to build schools, day-care centers, and railroads, house the homeless, fight racism, and care for the poor and elderly.

Many Plowshare activists are devout Catholics, but most Americans practice some form of religion, and even many of the jurors who convict and judges who sentence Plowshare activists concede they would like to see the world's nations beat swords into plowshares. Indeed, prosecutors who demand prison sentences for people like the Berrigans will confide that they also want peace on earth. The real issue, they say, is not whether the arms race is right or wrong, but whether any nation can allow its citizens to violate laws with which they disagree. Were they able to, the collective agreements that bind our society together would soon unravel.

To this argument, Daniel Berrigan replies that nuclear weapons are no more sacrosanct than the gas chambers at Auschwitz, no more entitled to legal protection than the freight trains that hauled six million Jews to their deaths. Our laws, say Plowshare activists, serve not to protect the world community from nuclear genocide, but to legitimize, even enshrine, the means of our destruction.

And while American and Soviet officials work hard and, apparently, with considerable success to persuade their citizens that the arms race will soon end, Plowshare activists point out that our own weapons factories are building three to ten new warheads every day, our scientists have continued their efforts to design a scientific anti-ballistic shield (Star Wars), and both superpowers continue underground testing of atomic weapons. Moreover, in spite of the waning of the Cold War, U.S. officials refuse the Soviet Union's offer to sign a "no-first-strike" agreement, and will not agree to eliminate atomic weapons from the high seas. Like a cancer that's treated one minute only to be fed growth hormones the next, our stockpiles of warheads *appear* to diminish, only to grow again in a more sophisticated, clandestine, and deadly manner. In our efforts to protect ourselves from our enemies, says Philip Berrigan, we may have despoiled our environment irrevocably with radioactive isotopes and carcinogenic plutonium.

At the very least, Plowshare activists are controversial figures whose ultimate judge will be history. Dismissed by the

Pentagon as the Pied Pipers of the peace movement's lunatic fringe, labeled arrogant and called terrorists by federal judges, praised by jurors who sentence them to prison, and rejected as fanatics and doomsayers by some of their fellow peace activists, they remain faithful to their belief that people must take direct nonviolent action to beat swords into plowshares. In a world bristling with weapons, the Plowshare Movement's message is of hope. In a nation where Newspeak and jabberwocky have replaced the language of common sense, Plowshare activists try to speak truthfully. And on a planet being stripped of its life-sustaining natural resources by government-supported greed, they choose to live simply and, in some cases, in poverty.

If what the Berrigans and others are saying is true, and if we fail to change our ways, the human race will disappear and there will be no one to decide whether the ideas and actions of the Plowshare movement really matter. On the other hand, should the superpowers decide to truly disarm—not to make sleight-of-hand agreements allowing each country to maintain enough warheads (six thousand each) to destroy the world several times over—then it will be most interesting to see how much credit, if any, Plowshare activists will be given for bringing about world peace.

My own sense is that one day our grandchildren and great-grandchildren will study Plowshare activists as we now do Harriet Tubman, Sojourner Truth, Martin Luther King, Jr., and Mahatma Gandhi. They too were greatly loved and passionately hated while they lived, a fate reserved for all uncommon martyrs.

# Notes

1. Arthur J. Laffin and Anne Montgomery, eds., *Swords Into Plowshares.* (New York: Harper & Row, 1987), 55.

# Uncommon
# Martyrs

# One

## In the Land of Burning Children

A prophet is not without honor, save in his
own country, and in his own house.

MATTHEW XIII, 46

As a boy growing up on Minnesota's Iron Range, Daniel Berrigan would lie in bed at night, listening to the wolves' baleful singing. Wind pounded through the trees, rocking the plank-and-tarpaper house like a cradle. The wolves sang a cappella dirges, odes to their own heroic past, or simple taunts to their human enemies. But unlike other boys his age, Daniel did not wish to kill them, dreaming instead of riding with them across the frozen tundra. He would hold his wolf-steed's ears for reins, galloping by his astonished brothers, leaping over his angry father, blowing kisses to his delighted mother. Like St. Francis of Assisi, he would call the great beasts to him and, stroking their powerful heads with infinite compassion and love, gaze into their melancholy green eyes.

In the early 'twenties, northern Minnesota was still pioneer country, where Scandinavian immigrants, arriving with little more than a set of clothes and a well-honed axe, built homesteads beside a thousand streams and lakes. Like most of their neighbors, the Berrigans were hard-working but poor, living always on a slim margin of survival. To support his wife and six sons, Tom Berrigan worked as a farmer, plumber, electrician, and railroad engineer, moving back and forth across the Iron Range in search of work and, it seems, himself. An Irishman straight from the works of Joyce and O'Neill, Dan's father was generous and envious, bitter and boastful, champion of the working class at large, authoritarian tyrant at home. In the morning he might bully, even brawl, with his sons, only to sit them down after supper for a recital of poetry. Standing tall, his face still covered with cuts and bruises, he would intone Shakespeare, Yeats, Wordsworth, and Keats from memory, throwing in an epic or two of his own. Throughout his life he seemed to be an angry Don Quixote, tilting at the very things and people he most loved.

The second-youngest of six brothers, Daniel was smaller than the rest, a disappointment to his father, who could not abide human illness or weakness. By the age of four, Dan was still not walking, his ankles too weak to carry even such a frail body. In the wilds of northern Minnesota there were no orthopedic clinics, and the family could never afford expensive shoes or corrective operations. But Dan's maternal grandmother, who'd immigrated from Germany and lived with the family, insisted he would walk. With a pair of high-button shoes reinforced "like a ship's hull, with struts of whalebone," he would soon be running in the snow with his brothers. Each day, Dan's grandmother would carry him into the yard, massaging his feet in the meager and fleeting sunlight until the weak bones slowly took shape. The boy hobbled, then walked. One afternoon, Dan's grandmother heard loud screaming outside the kitchen. Alarmed, she looked out to see a fox (Dan) chasing a flock of geese (his brothers) through the snow. The fox fell, rose, fell again, clutching the tailfeathers of a very agile goose.

Of his mother, Dan would later write that she was the kind of woman who could be entrusted with the fate of the world. On the Iron Range, women, and sometimes entire families, broke from the strain of poverty and endless hard work. Six ravenous and mischievous boys, a flamboyant and tempestuous husband; backbreaking days over a washtub, bitter winter nights trying to stretch the beans and bread, macaroni and meatloaf, just another meal—yet Frieda Berrigan survived. Without her, said Berrigan, Tom's vitriolic fits and furious contradictions might have ruined his sons. The struggle took its toll on Frieda. Sometimes the boys would find her standing alone in the kitchen, tears streaking her cheeks. The years passed and her loneliness deepened, but she would not join the women's card-and-gossip club, preferring to read during precious moments of leisure. And, long before the feminist movement, she quietly defied her husband's domination in ways that he most likely failed to see.

Two years younger than Daniel, Philip Berrigan seemed to have sprung into the world from a Wheaties box. Strong and handsome, quick with his fists, athletic, he was a star baseball and basketball player in high school. Yet both brothers were intensely interested in books and ideas, avid readers of the works their mother brought home from the library. Frieda urged them to read *Lives of the Saints* and the Old and New Testaments, as well as their father's magazines—*Commonweal*, a liberal Catholic journal, and the *Catholic Worker*, a small newspaper in which Dorothy Day and others wrote about working among New York's poor.

Shortly after the stock market collapsed in 1929, Tom Berrigan was fired for being a member of the militant Socialist Party. The family moved to a ten-acre farm outside Syracuse, New York. On the shores of Lake Onondaga, new electrical plants were being built, and Tom managed to find work there. As the Depression deepened, many workers, fearful of retaliation from employers, kept quiet about their political affiliations. But Tom Berrigan would not live in fear, founding Syracuse's Electrical Workers' Union and the Catholic Interracial Council, activities almost revolutionary for those times.

Ragged and hungry travelers began appearing at the Berrigans' door, and regardless of how little food the family might have, no one was ever turned away. Seated around the table, the Berrigan brothers would watch their parents divide the evening meal like loaves and fishes, then parcel it out equally to family and strangers. On some nights the Berrigans' guests told strange, frightening stories of families being forced from their homes, their furniture smashed and children hauled away, of babies and old folks dying of malnutrition, of people who'd been driven out of their minds with suffering placing a shotgun to their own foreheads. And even stranger: great mounds of oranges were being doused with kerosene in California and set afire; in some cities, restaurants were dumping creosote on their garbage so people couldn't eat it; in the hobo jungles and Hoovervilles, vigilantes were beating up the unemployed, then burning down their shacks.

The boys listened, trying fully to comprehend these cruelties and hardships. In a Christian nation, they asked, how could such things happen? In a Christian nation, their father roared, such things would not.

After graduating from high school, Philip took a job scrubbing engines in a railroad roundhouse and played first base on a semiprofessional baseball team in order to earn money for college. In the fall of 1942, he enrolled in St. Michael's College in Toronto, realizing that his studies might soon end. The United States was at war with Germany and Japan, and before the conflict ended four of the six Berrigan brothers would serve in the military. Daniel was in a seminary, studying to be a priest. In high school he'd written to all of the Catholic religious orders, and had chosen the Jesuits, who replied with a simple pamphlet making no promises and containing little more than a few quotes from Saint Ignatius.

The Jesuits had a tumultuous and controversial history. Members of the order had taught Racine, Corneille, Moliere, Descartes, Diderot, Voltaire, and Lamartine. They had served as spiritual directors to kings and princes, and had been banished by Queen Elizabeth, who accused them of conspiring against the Church of England. They'd been expelled from Portugal in 1759, from France in 1762. At least one of their members, Father Edmund Campion, had been condemned for high treason, then hanged and quartered. Fathers Marquette, Joliet, Dolbeau, and Albanel were explorers. Fathers Brebeuf, Lalemant, Bressani, and Daniel were scalped and burned at the stake. "I became a Jesuit," Daniel Berrigan would tell friends and reporters, "because they had a revolutionary history. I only suspected it at the time; now I am more certain, and more proud."[1] Four times a year Frieda and Tom were allowed to visit their son, but it would be seven years before he could visit the family farmstead again.

Philip Berrigan was nineteen when he entered the army.

Three of his brothers were already fighting in the war, and driving through the ruins of Britain's great cities Philip's unit gathered supplies as they prepared to move out to the European front. The smoke had cleared and the fires gone out, but Philip found the rubble deeply troubling, the bombed-out schools and burned-out hospitals a sudden ending to any romantic illusions he might have had about war. Two months after D-Day, Philip's unit swept into France to liquidate the resistance around Brest and other cities where the Nazis were dug deep into fortifications. On across France with the First and Ninth armies, down through Holland, into the Ruhr valley, the landscape pocked and scarred, the roads clogged with refugees, skeletons of tanks and trucks, and dead and dying humans. After fifteen months in Europe, Berrigan was to return to Fort Leonard Wood, Missouri, to be trained for the invasion of Japan but on August 7, 1945, the United States dropped *Little Boy* on Hiroshima. A few days later, *Fat Man* exploded over Nagasaki.

Years later, Philip would look back on his support of the bombing with great sadness and regret. He had accepted Harry Truman's explanation that the atom bomb saved American lives, discovering only later that the Japanese were all but defeated when *Little Boy* fell on Hiroshima. Before surrendering the Japanese had wanted some assurance on the status of Emperor Hirohito—a status Gen. Douglas MacArthur had already guaranteed when the atomic bomb was dropped. Men, women, and children had been burned alive not to end the war, but to prove a point to the Soviet Union and the world. In the mushroom clouds that rose over Nagasaki and Hiroshima, an empire had been born, one whose leaders would not hesitate in the future to threaten the use of atomic weapons to gain their foreign policy objectives.

Returning from the war, Philip enrolled in Holy Cross and after graduation joined the Josephite order of priests, missionaries to blacks in the U.S. Happy days, with evil conquered in Europe and the U.S. growing more prosperous and powerful each day. But on May 17, 1954, the U.S. Supreme Court shattered this postwar serenity by ruling that in public education the "doctrine of 'separate but equal' has no place. Separate educational facilities are inherently unequal." To segregationists, the ruling meant far more than the distant possibility of white and black children attending school together. *Brown* v. *the Board of Education,* they said, was the death knell of the American way of life, the passing of all that was noble and chivalrous, the beginning of "interbreeding" that would mean the demise of the human (white) race. By gun, rope, firebomb, random torture and well-orchestrated terror, integration would be resisted.

As racist violence spread, Philip, who was teaching in an all-black high school in New Orleans, could not escape a growing, at times almost overwhelming, sense of irony. Just a few years before he and hundreds of thousands of U.S. citizens had risked their lives to defeat the Nazis, yet here in America black people were forced to live in segregated housing, attend separate schools, and work at the most menial, low-paying jobs. How, he wondered, could a Christian stand by and watch such things happen?

For Philip Berrigan this question was of critical importance. Certainly it was easy to talk about injustice while sitting in someone's comfortable living room, out of range of the nightsticks and tear gas. But was it really enough to talk about the plight of the poor, or victims of racial injustice, in the safety of one's own well-feathered nest? Would anything change if he and others simply wrote polite letters to the powerful, asking them to change their ways when the petitioners did not have the courage to change their own?

Berrigan marched in Selma and Montgomery, worked on voter registration drives, and recruited his students to picket segregated restaurants, for which he was reprimanded by his superiors. Soon he would become the best known priest in the civil rights movement, crisscrossing the South to speak out against racism. Daniel Berrigan had recently returned from France, where in the early 'fifties many Catholic priests had given up the comforts of the rectory to live and labor side-by-side with the workers. To express their belief that Christians must work for social justice, "worker priests" were living among the poor, marching in demonstrations, and joining strikes for better living conditions and higher wages. But the movement was short-lived. Alarmed by the prospect of priests marching arm-in-arm with avowed Communists, French bishops denounced the worker-priest movement. In January 1954, Pope Pius XII, warning against the "spirit of innovation," ordered the worker priests to leave the factories, agricultural areas, and fishing fleets, and return to more traditional parish work. Refusing these orders, he warned, would lead to excommunication. All but a few complied. In the streets of France's war-ravaged cities, on the docks, and in the fields, Berrigan had seen Catholic priests living out what they believed to be the true message of the Gospels: serving the poor, liberating the oppressed, a life of voluntary poverty. And for the first—but by no means the last—time, he had seen how summarily church officials would respond to anyone who tried to practice, not just preach, the example of Jesus.

Back in the U.S., Dan was given a three-year teaching assignment at Brooklyn Preparatory, a time he would later recall as a "heyday among Catholics." It was exciting to read and debate articles that appeared in *Integrity* and *Jubilee, Commonweal* and the *Catholic Worker,* a great pleasure to take his students on regular trips to the Lower East Side, where they would work at the Nativity Center, welcoming the newest wave of Puerto Rican immigrants to the U.S. On other occasions, they would visit the Catholic Worker to observe firsthand the voluntary poverty and social activism of Dorothy Day and friends. In 1957, Daniel Berrigan's first book of poems, *Time Without Number,* was published to considerable critical acclaim, winning the Lamont Poetry Prize and nominated for the National Book Award. That same year, he was appointed a Professor of Religion at Le Moyne College in Syracuse.

At Le Moyne, Dan established an off-campus house where students and teachers could meet informally to talk about and debate the real meaning of being a Christian. Could it be, Dan would ask, that the church suffers from a kind of moral schizophrenia, stating one thing in its doctrines while practicing quite another? In response, Dan's students began working with ghetto residents to organize rent strikes, picket businesses that practiced discrimination, and challenge their clergy to join the struggle for social justice. Criticism of his actions mounted, but if Father Berrigan heard the muttering in the chancery or the whispering in departmental offices, he chose to ignore it. Nevertheless, tension between Dan and his superiors increased when his request to go on a freedom ride was denied, and culminated when he was asked to take a year's sabbatical from the college. For Daniel this was the first crisis with his order, and a harbinger of further controversy.

Philip was still working in the South when President Kennedy demanded that the Soviet Union dismantle several missile sites its technicians were constructing in Cuba. Nikita Khrushchev balked and the world hovered near the brink of destruction, leaned over and peered into the abyss. As the superpowers exchanged warnings and threats, some Americans went abroad, hoping to escape atomic war. Others held farewell parties or fled the South in order to be out of the missiles' range.

The standoff between Kennedy and Khrushchev finally ended, but Philip could not stop thinking about the millions of people who would die during the first hour of an atomic war. How many Coventrys, Rotterdams, and Hiroshimas would that be? Assuming there were survivors to perform such tasks, where would all the dead be buried? Why had John Kennedy risked destroying the world? No one had asked the American or Soviet people if they wanted to see their towns and cities vaporized in order to prove their system was the best. No plebiscite, in fact, had ever been taken to determine if people wanted to use nuclear weapons as an instrument of foreign policy. Long before there was any real opposition to the arms race, Philip Berrigan realized that the fate of the earth was in the hands of a few powerful men whose obsessive need to be right could mean the end of the world.

Philip began to research the Cold War, stuffing strips of paper into books to mark significant passages, underlining, dogearing, shaking his head as he realized that the U.S. was preparing for Armageddon and that few people were trying to stop it. Cartoonists depicted those who did protest as scruffy, wild-eyed lunatics waving signs scrawled with apocalyptic messages. Berrigan was well aware of the agreement Pope Pius XII had made with Adolf Hitler in 1933 not to interfere with the Nazis if they, in turn, left the Catholic church alone. He had read about and agonized over the official church's silence while millions of Jews, gypsies, homosexuals, Communists, and socialists were rounded up and sent off to die in concentration camps. And now, as the superpowers were testing weapons that would make the Hiroshima bomb look like a firecracker, history seemed to be repeating itself. As it had done all too often, the official church remained silent, accepting and even openly supporting war and injustice.

If the 'sixties were rung in on a note of euphoria, the good mood soon dissipated into the sounds of assassins' bullets, anti-war chants, exploding tear-gas cannisters and double-barreled shotguns. Like some science-fiction virus, violence swept across the American landscape, killing John F. Kennedy, Medgar Evers, Malcolm X, Martin Luther King, Jr., Robert Kennedy, and many others. "Violence," said civil rights activist and black militant H. Rap Brown, "is as American as cherry pie." White Americans were outraged. Black Americans only nodded, their individual and collective experience a confirmation of Brown's simile. The killing spread across the Pacific. Like Detroit, Newark, and Watts, Vietnam began to burn. Waves of B-52s pounded schools, hospitals, day-care centers; C-123s doused the roadsides and jungles with Agent Orange; hundreds of thousands of young Americans were dispatched to fight for the "sovereign nation of South Vietnam." The war at home expanded. Blacks against whites. Young against old. Hawks against doves.

Dan and Philip Berrigan had come to know and greatly admire Dorothy Day, peace activist, pacifist, co-founder of the *Catholic Worker*, and uncompromising critic of the greed and avarice that, she said, oiled and fueled the American war machine. "She came to see," Daniel would later write in tribute, "that, in America, human devastation was by no means fortuitous; it was embedded in the scheme and texture of the social contract, like rods of steel reinforced, prestressing the dead weight of life."[2] For Dorothy Day there were no exceptions to *Thou Shalt Not Kill*, no footnotes or razor's-edge evasions. Christians must say no to war, any war, all wars, always, and Vietnam was no exception. The war must be resisted absolutely, nonviolently, even if this meant loss of status, friends, and jobs; even if it meant going to prison for years.

An "enthusiastic participant" in World War II, Philip was now going through a spiritual conversion. According to church doctrine, war could be justified if:

- it is declared by legitimate authority
- it is a defensive war waged against an unjust aggressor
- all peaceful remedies have been exhausted before resorting to war
- the lives of innocents and noncombatants are protected
- it follows the "principle of proportionality," meaning that the methods used to wage war are no crueler or more oppressive than the evil to be remedied[3]

Invited to speak to high school and college classes, Philip Berrigan told his listeners that the Vietnam War met none of these criteria.

"Our support of the Saigon government," Berrigan would thunder, "which is, in reality, no government; our indiscriminate attacks with bombs and napalm against innocent peasants in the hope of killing a few Viet Cong; our bombing of industry and transportation in a nation against whom we have no cause for grievance, and against whom we have not declared war; our testing of inhumane weapons and the increasing troop commitment to a combat role; the whole rising tide of savagery and ruin which we have provoked and which we now sustain—these not only contradict the Gospel and make fidelity to it a mockery, they also reject, out of hand, the theory of the Just War . . ."[4]

Philip would also speak about the connections between racism and military expenditures, telling his audiences that if the government really cared about black people it would spend taxpayers' money to build schools and hospitals, not atomic weapons. Berrigan would announce to his astonished and, in many cases, skeptical listeners that throughout the world, and even in the United States, children were starving because our government would rather plan for war than plant seeds, preferred to spend its money on missiles rather than windmills, and seemed to hate the poor and disenfranchised, the very people Jesus told us we must love. Twenty years later, it would not be that uncommon to hear a priest say such things; but, at the time, Berrigan's message was both astonishing and prophetic, a mark of his own alienation from mainstream Catholicism and from many if not most of his fellow countrymen and women. Most disturbing was that Berrigan had joined the ranks of some of

our nation's most controversial figures—naturalist Henry
David Thoreau; union leader Eugene Debs; clergyman A. J.
Muste; poet Robert Lowell; Catholic convert Dorothy Day;
and writer, teacher, and activist David Dellinger—Americans
who had defied cultural tradition and the teachings of the
church by insisting that war could never be just. In the tradition of some of our most misunderstood figures, said Berrigan, he had decided to repudiate all war, to live out the rest
of his life as a pacifist.

Assigned to Newburgh, New York, Philip promptly began
working with a group of seminarians to set up a *Catholic
Worker* storefront operation to distribute food and clothing
to the poor. In driving snow or bitter upstate rain, Berrigan
and friends stood in front of City Hall, their picket signs demanding an end to racism. When city officials refused to respond, Berrigan's group divided into investigative teams,
scouring the ghetto to determine the type and number of
housing violations in each building. As Berrigan's fame
grew, so too did the vehemence of his critics, who mounted
a letter and phone-in campaign to convince Berrigan's superiors that he was a dangerous man, leading the civil rights
movement and his students toward the wasteland of international Communism. Summoned to the chancery one
afternoon, Philip was informed he must leave Newburgh,
New York, a decision he heralded as a victory for the anti-
war and civil rights movements, rather than as a personal
defeat. Day and night, journalists phoned to ask for interviews, and priests called to express their support. The liberal
Catholic press soon picked up the story, proclaiming Berrigan's ouster in banner headlines and describing his anti-war
efforts in considerable detail. With each new rebuke from

the hierarchy, support for Dan and Phil was growing among the more liberal clergy.

To mainstream Catholics the Berrigans were Socratic gadflies, beguiling the young with strange and dangerous ideas about what it means to be a Christian, insisting that there has never been and will never be a just war, arguing that killing can never be justified, encouraging young men to resist the draft, demanding not just an end to the fighting in Southeast Asia but the beginning of a new, nonviolent consciousness. To many people the most frightening thing about the Berrigans was not what they said, but their utter indifference to the comforts of American life. Highly educated, talented writers and brilliant theologians, the Berrigans could easily have acquired wealth and fame. Instead, they chose to live simply, working with the poor and disenfranchised, refusing to own property, and living in community with people who were dedicating their lives to fighting racism, ending the Vietnam War, and stopping the arms race. A quarter-century later, they continue to live in voluntary poverty: owning no property, giving what they have to the less fortunate, risking their lives and going to prison for their beliefs.

By 1964, Daniel Berrigan had returned from European exile and was working once again in New York. In Eastern Europe, Dan had met Christians who risked jail and other forms of punishment to practice their faith, men and women, he would tell supporters, who had been abandoned by the West and their own church. In South Africa, Berrigan had observed the suffering of blacks under apartheid and, when invited to preach to an all-white congregation, told the parishioners that "God abhors the crime of silence." At another gathering, a young mother had asked Father Berrigan what would become of the children if she and others were arrested for opposing apartheid. "Under such circumstances," Berrigan responded, "what will become of our children if we don't?"

In 1964, Daniel, Philip, Thomas Merton, and members of New York's *Catholic Worker* movement, founded the Catholic Peace Fellowship, the first Catholic anti-war organization in the country. Dan was editing *Jesuit Missions* and trying to find time to spend at least one day a week ladling soup to the homeless or handing out free clothes at the *Catholic Worker* on Crystie Street. President Johnson was waging "war on poverty" in America's ghettos, but to Dan and friends it was becoming increasingly clear that the real war was twelve thousand miles away in the rice paddies and jungles of Vietnam. In 1965, the Marines landed at Danang, and President Johnson launched Operation Rolling Thunder, an attempt to bomb the North Vietnamese into submission. To assure support for the war, administration officials began a calculated effort to deceive the American people, a pattern of governmental duplicity, say the Berrigans and friends, that continues to this day.

As the war escalated, so did the opposition. On October 15, 1965, a young man stood in front of the Armed Forces Induction Center in downtown Manhattan. In his clean, well-pressed suit and narrow tie, he might have been an aspiring executive or stockbroker, one of hundreds of young men who appeared each day for pre-induction physicals. But instead of entering the center, David Miller held a small white piece of paper aloft and torched one corner with a cigarette lighter. Cameras flashed, a few people clapped, and others seemed to be in shock. To government officials, setting fire to a draft card was similar to burning the American flag. For his act of defiance, the very first public burning of a draft card in the United States, David Miller was given a three-year sentence in a federal penitentiary.

Asked by reporters how they felt about Miller's action, Fathers Philip and Daniel Berrigan replied that nonviolent defiance of the Vietnam War was not only noble, but absolutely necessary. Moreover, resistance to injustices like slavery, economic exploitation, and war was very much in the American grain. David Miller was acting in the best tradition of abolitionists like William Lloyd Garrison, emancipators like Harriet Tubman, and "dangerous revolutionaries" like Samuel Adams, Patrick Henry, and Thomas Paine. As U.S. citizens, Catholic priests, and Christians, said Dan and Phil, we wholeheartedly support breaking the law if it helps end the killing in Southeast Asia. Three weeks after Miller's arrest, a young *Catholic Worker* activist and former seminarian, Roger Laporte, sat down on the steps of the United Nations, emptied a gallon jug of gasoline over his body and struck a match, an act immediately labeled a suicide by New York's archdiocese. Daniel Berrigan's superiors warned him that under no circumstances was he to make a public statement regarding Laporte's death. But when requested to speak to those attending a memorial service for Laporte at the *Catholic Worker*, Dan asked whether the young man's death wasn't more than an ordinary suicide. Indeed, he asked if Laporte's action might have reflected something more than despair. Might it be possible to see hope in his act, rather than merely condemning the deceased to moral judgment? "His death was offered," said Daniel Berrigan, "so that others might live."

Reaction to Dan's participation in the memorial service was swift, uncompromising, and cruel. In the fall of 1965, he received notice from Cardinal Spellman's chancery that he was to pack his bags and depart posthaste for Latin America. Where? No destination given. His return? No answer provided. A visit to his sick and aging parents, perhaps? Forbidden. The orders were clear, direct, impossible to misinterpret. Get out of town. Don't come back. "And," said Berrigan, still obviously hurt so many years later, "those Jesuits wouldn't receive me anywhere, you know, including the community in Syracuse where I had labored for six years. Everyone was saying, 'Get lost,' slamming doors. Oh, it was unbelievable. But I think . . . well, you know, it was very important, because I tasted pariah. I really tasted crow."

Thus Dan Berrigan began yet another exile, this time to Cuernavaca, Caracas, and São Paulo, where he would observe the misery in which the poor lived and died. He moved from country to country, city to city, deeply touched by the suffering in the urban slums, neither surprised nor depressed by collusion between the church and dictatorial governments, greatly inspired by the worker priests who were willing to sacrifice their comforts and even their lives to help impoverished urban dwellers and *campesinos*. Vacillating between despair and inspiration, tormented by doubt and self-pity, tempted at times to leave the church altogether, Dan wandered in and out of spiritual turmoil. Yet what he learned would instruct his vision and inspire his quest for social justice in the years to come.

If the church expected Daniel Berrigan to stumble blindly through the fields of misery, not seeing the reality of imperialism—lifelong poverty, starvation, economic slavery, early death—its leadership had made a terrible mistake. Dan Berrigan would not only survive his exile, but would return to the states with a passionate and unbreakable commitment to the poor. For the next quarter-century, he and Philip would write, lecture, and go to jail for their belief that, in a world where 50,000 people starve needlessly each day, "war is blasphemy." In a world where nation states spend millions every hour preparing for battle while tens of millions of children go to bed hungry every night, *war is an obscenity.*

Daniel Berrigan quietly sips his coffee. He looks so much older now, the skin over his cheekbones deeply lined, his hair grey, and rather ominous-looking spots beneath his eyes. In the streets below, the endless Manhattan honking. I recall the first time I met him. The Vietnam War was raging, and scenes of napalmed children, stacks of body bags, silver coffins fork-lifted into cavernous aircraft, dead Vietnamese, dead Americans, dead students at Kent and Jackson state universities were nightly fare on the evening news. We were waiting for him at the home of Mary Bye, a Quaker peace activist whose numerous arrests and incarcerations were legend in Bucks County, Pennsylvania. It was a warm day, pale cloudless sky, the crowd sipping tea and freshly pressed apple cider, wandering through Bye's estate or standing about in excited little clusters. Closing my eyes I could almost hear the stamen winesaps and pears ripening, the ash and maple trees changing color. Children could not be burning, peasants and young Americans dying on a day like this.

Mary Bye's guest shattered my reverie and the crowd's good mood. It was nice to see us, said Berrigan, but sipping cider on a grand Bucks County afternoon was really rather pointless. It was great to be out of jail, he said, but if we really wanted the killing to stop in Southeast Asia we would have to do more, far more, than come out to hear a radical chic celebrity. Enough talk, said the little man in a black turtleneck. Enough excuses. Enough of, "Oh, I really can't break the law because my friends might think I'm too extreme . . . family will disown . . . church might condemn . . ." Such things, said Bye's guest, could hardly matter when children were burning. . . . Close your eyes for a moment. . . . Listen to their cries. . . .

Not a comforting homily, and hardly the kind of congratulations Bye's guests expected to hear. And there was more, even when the crowd began to break like an ice floe at the edges, the soft-spoken words challenging and alienating. We stood in the sunshine listening to this peculiar little man, a Jeremiah one moment, a Jesuit Lenny Bruce (without profanity) the next, with the Celtic humor and keen sense of irony that has produced so many great Irish writers and orators. The crowd listened and squirmed a bit, then headed for home, pleased to have had an audience with this notorious rabble-rouser but convinced that even in the land of burning children, a glass of scotch and a hot bath were preferable to prison.

The next thing I heard about Daniel Berrigan was that, after refusing to surrender to the federal marshals, he'd been captured on August 12, 1970, on Block Island, Rhode Island. A photograph, flashed around the world at the time, shows Father Berrigan flanked by two very pugnacious-looking FBI agents. He is wearing a rain slicker, slacks, and sneakers. His hands are cuffed in front of him, and he is grinning, not at all like a man who will spend the next two and a half years in prison.

# Notes

1. Francine du Plessix Gray, *Divine Disobedience* (New York: Vintage, 1969), 109.

# Two

## Prophets and Pariahs

Daniel Berrigan returned from exile as a hero to his supporters and a recalcitrant troublemaker to those who had sent him away. He had withstood Cardinal Spellman's attempts to break his spirit, and was now more determined than ever to speak out against the war in Vietnam. During his absence, there had been a substantial and—to the church hierarchy—surprising outpouring of support for Berrigan from liberal Catholics. *Commonweal* called his forced exile a "shame and a scandal, a disgustingly blind totalitarian act." The *National Catholic Reporter* criticized the chancery. The *New York Times* published the reaction of Dan's friends and supporters, and seminary students from Fordham University marched in front of the residence of the archbishop of New York carrying signs that read:

END POWER POLITICS IN THE CHURCH
EXILE AND CONSTRAINT ARE THE TOOLS OF TOTALITARIANISM
SAINT PAUL WAS A REBEL

In the early months of 1967, two staff members from Cornell University's United Religious Work arrived in Manhattan to ask Daniel to join their staff. His duties would include counseling students, holding worship services, and teaching a literature course or two. Thus, in the spring, Daniel began teaching courses in modern drama and the New Testament at Cornell University, a Wordsworthian setting where he could stop on his way to work and listen to water cascading through the gorges, robins and cardinals heralding the end of winter, students laughing and chattering about exams and love affairs, professors feared, hated, and admired. How easy to remain in this idyllic setting, to sit upon a warm stone, his feet dangling in the cool rushing water, sunlight cascading through the trees, with some wine and cheese and a good book perched upon his lap. To pretend that the napalm canisters and phosphorus bombs weren't falling. To shut out the sounds and banish the sights of death. Go for tenure. Walk softly. Sleep late. Publish. Invite friends to gourmet dinners. Exorcise the knowledge that we are all responsible for the killing. Forget what his friend and confidant Thomas Merton had written:

> But who are "we"? We are the intellectuals who have taken for granted that we could be "bystanders" and that our quality as detached observers could preserve our innocence and relieve us of responsibility. . . . A witness of a crime, who just stands by and makes a mental note of the fact he is an innocent bystander, tends by that very fact to become an accomplice.[1]

That summer, Philip arrived on the Cornell campus with a bold, innovative, and, to Daniel, deeply troubling plan. It was imperative, said Philip, that the anti-war movement go beyond sit-ins and teach-ins. Marching and singing, petitioning and praying should continue, but more must be done to stop this savage war. Philip explained that he and a few friends had decided to walk into a draft board in Baltimore, Maryland, pour blood on the files, and then simply wait there for the police to arrive, accepting whatever consequences there might be. The draft board invasion would be consistent with the spirit of King and Gandhi: nonviolent, loving, wholeheartedly in the name of peace. Still, Dan and Phil realized, what they were discussing would be a shift not only in thought but in action, a leap into the cauldron of controversy, with the real possibility they would be misunderstood, ridiculed, even condemned, by the church, fellow peace activists, and friends.

Daniel declined his brother's offer, explaining that he would stay on at Cornell, doing what he could to support young students who were working for peace and social justice. Philip was impatient. He and other members of the clergy had already tried hard to approach government officials, picketing the homes of the Joint Chiefs of Staff, demonstrating in front of Secretary of State Dean Rusk's home, and praying on Secretary of Defense Robert McNamara's lawn. Philip Berrigan had been invited to meet with Rusk, but left the meeting even more convinced that talking to the architects of the Vietnam War was futile. What was needed, he told friends, was something new, bold, creative. Something, said Berrigan, like the courageous actions of Catholic priests who had resisted Hitler, knowing the consequences would be prison or death.

On October 27, 1967, shortly before noon, Philip Berrigan; James Mengel, a former army chaplain of the United Church of Christ; Tom Lewis, artist and devout Catholic; and David Eberhardt, poet and agnostic, walked into the Customs House in Baltimore, Maryland, and through a door to the Selective Service Office, where they poured blood over files containing the names of draft-eligible males. Clerks screamed, and the press, tipped off that the action was going to occur, snapped pictures. Within a minute it was over, and the raiders sat down outside the office, waiting to be taken away by the FBI.

If the Catholic church had become, in the words of Daniel Berrigan, "a holy morgue," with the dead preaching to catatonic parishioners, the Baltimore Four's action would shake the dead out of their comfortable slumber. Many Catholics wrote to Dan and Phil insisting that the Vietnam War was just, moral, consistent with the teachings of the church, and in the very best interests of the state. Furthermore, said the Berrigans' critics, priests belonged in the parish, at weddings and funerals, baptisms and confessions. Priests ought to be at the side of those who, regardless of the cause, are fighting for our nation. Blood on draft files: *Outrageous.* Damaging public property: *Stupid.* Breaking the law: *Absolutely embarrassing to Catholics, to the mother church, to Christians everywhere. Priests who did such things should be censored, chastised, sent to prison, defrocked.*

Mengel and Eberhardt left jail after a day or two, but Philip and Tom Lewis fasted in their cells for a week. On April 1, 1968, the trial of Berrigan and friends commenced in a federal courthouse in Baltimore, Maryland. Those who expected the four to plea-bargain, show contrition, or concede they'd made a serious political and theological *faux pas* were mistaken. Instead of promising never to do such a thing again, Philip and friends were unrepentant, even proud. The judge shook his head in dismay, jurors murmured, and the media rushed to and fro, firing off stories about this most peculiar group, the "Catholic Left."

The war in Vietnam, said the Baltimore Four, was a crime against humanity, a genocide comparable to what the Nazis had done to the Jews. No man or woman could stand by and watch it happen and still call him/herself a Christian. No church could support such massive violence and still insist that it spoke with moral authority—about anything. Yes, said the defendants, they were glad they'd poured blood on these "hunting licenses against humans." They had no regrets, would probably do it again, and were prepared to accept the consequences. When the jury handed down its guilty verdict, Philip Berrigan became the first priest in U.S. history to be tried, convicted, and sent to prison for a political crime.

Although few people understood, something profound and irrevocable was taking place in that supercharged Baltimore courtroom. Cast out from the moral certitude and political consensus of church and state, the Baltimore Four were demanding that the "peacemaking Jesus" replace swashbuckling bishops and combat-booted cardinals as the moral leader of the Catholic church. Four Americans, one of them a combat veteran of World War II and a member of the Josephite order of priests, were making a radical break with their nation's mythology by suggesting that, like other countries, the U.S. could behave cruelly, even criminally, to secure its foreign policy goals. Citizens, said Berrigan *et al.*, had not only the right but a God-given duty to oppose violence, challenge church authority, expose hypocrisy, and follow the Christ of love instead of the gods of war.

Twelve years before the first official Plowshare action, the groundwork had been established for new forms of resistance to state violence, and to the church which, Plowshare activists argue, serves as the state's protector. In his writings from prison, Philip Berrigan would acknowledge the influence of Henry David Thoreau on his thinking and actions. The state, said Thoreau, might convict, sentence, imprison, and even kill a citizen but it could never defeat someone who truly stands up for justice. Indeed, the more the state corrupts and manipulates its courts, conspires to jail and murder its critics, the less legitimate it becomes, until finally any real hope for its future is lost. He declared:

> The mass of men serve the state thus: not as men mainly, but as machines, with their bodies. They are the standing army, and the militia, jailers, constables, posse comitatus, &c. In most cases there is no free exercise whatever of the judgment or of the moral sense; but they put themselves on a level with wood and earth and stones; and wooden men can perhaps be manufactured that will serve the purpose as well . . . How does it become a man to behave toward this American government to-day? I answer, that he cannot without disgrace be associated with it. I cannot for an instant recognize that political organizations as *my* government which is the *slave's* government also.[2]

Thoreau spent only one night in a rather comfortable Concord jail for refusing to pay a poll tax, a part of which would have been used to support President Polk's colonialist war against Mexico. But for the Berrigans and others whose vision of the church and of the United States had been radically altered by the Vietnam War, working in inner-city ghettos and with the impoverished people of Latin America, resistance would be lifelong, the consequences measured by years of confinement in city, county, and federal jails.

In January 1968, as preparations for Philip's trial were being made, Daniel Berrigan and Boston University professor Howard Zinn were invited by a North Vietnamese peace delegation to escort three American fliers home as a gesture of good will on the Buddhist holiday of Tet. Both readily agreed, arriving in Hanoi just a few days after the Tet Offensive began in the south. Dan was meeting with lay members of the Vietnam Committee for Patriotic Catholics when the air-raid siren sounded, forcing them to take shelter in an underground bunker. A wave of B-52s dropped clusters of 1,000-pound bombs and the world rose and fell in slow motion, beads of sweat curling from Dan's armpits, tiny fly-feet down his back, under his belt, rage rising beyond his fear, to the point of bitter clarity. The State Department knew he and Professor Zinn were there. The Pentagon and White House knew. Was the U.S. government trying to sabotage its own efforts to free the fliers? Were U.S. officials trying to frighten—perhaps even *kill*—Berrigan and Zinn? Later, Dan would write that he emerged from the bunker deeply shaken and angry, yet with a new clarity of vision about the war. "Not only the enemy is ground under," he would write, "but regard for those who might be considered 'our own,' is nearly obliterated. We're giving day by a day a new twist to that knife in man's vitals known as 'total war.'"[3]

The three pilots were released to Berrigan and Zinn, and the five men left Hanoi together on a commercial airliner. But in Vientiane, Laos, the U.S. Ambassador, William Sullivan, boarded the plane "like a buccaneer" to demand that the pilots complete the trip home by military aircraft. Berrigan and Zinn stood fast, trying to explain that they had made certain promises to the North Vietnamese, promises which, if broken, might jeopardize the future of similar prisoner releases. The standoff continued for nearly an hour, resolved when the ranking officer among the POWs informed Berrigan that he was still a military man and, therefore, must follow orders. Ambassador Sullivan smiled, and the pilots rose, following him down the plane's steps and out to the tarmac where the press was waiting.

Daniel returned to Ithaca and began work on a book about his trip to North Vietnam. Cayuga Lake, filled with sailboats in summer, appeared empty and forlorn. The sky was a deep, mottled, grey. When it snowed, the campus was quiet and extraordinarily beautiful. Spring arrived at last, and Philip visited Dan again at Cornell. A joyous occasion, with Philip recently out of jail, awaiting his trial for the Baltimore Four action. A time to talk, reflect, share the love they felt for one another. A squirrel charged across their path, chattering wild challenges to a pursuing black labrador. Philip stopped to light a cigarette, drawing deeply, and the discussion continued. No, he said, jail had not intimidated him. Certainly he did not look forward to spending years in prison, but if that was the price for opposing this war, then so be it—he was more than willing. "The world," Philip began, quoting one of his and Dan's favorite passages from Albert Camus, "expects that Christians will speak out loud and clear, so that never a doubt, never the slightest doubt, could rise in the heart of the simplest man.

"The world expects that Christians will get away from abstractions and confront the blood-stained face which history has taken on today.

"The grouping we need is a grouping of men resolved to speak out clearly and to pay up personally."[4]

Like Daniel, Philip enjoyed a leisurely afternoon walk in the woods, their infrequent and always intense reunions, a glass of Irish whiskey and a song, even a bit of dancing now and again. And like his brother, he loved the church, even when it banished the peacemaking Jesus and condemned those who insisted that if Christ returned he would be carrying an olive branch rather than an M-16. A voracious reader, his public lectures always carefully thought out and documented, Philip argued that throughout U.S. history nothing of any real importance had been achieved without great struggle and sacrifice, even bloodshed. Just take a look at the American labor movement, he would tell his students—the most violent labor struggles in the history of the world, men and women fighting and dying for such basic rights as a safe work place, child-labor laws, a work day that didn't begin at dawn and end long after dusk. And the government's reaction to these demands? To infiltrate the unions with informers, to send in the police and the army to arrest, beat, and murder strikers, and to use the press to frighten and manipulate the public into believing that social reformers and union activists were anarchists and Communists.

Good Lord, Berrigan would cry, had it not been for courageous people like Big Bill Haywood, Elizabeth Gurley Flynn, and William Trautmann, ten-year-old children would still be slaving sixteen hours a day in textile factories and dying at an early age from tuberculosis, malnutrition, and exhaustion. Had striking coal miners at Coeur d'Alene, Leadville, Salt Lake City, Idaho Spring, and Cripple Creek been unwilling to go without food and risk their jobs and their lives, they would still be working for starvation wages in water up to their knees, in mines that periodically caught fire, caved in, and blew up. And slavery? Nothing more than institutionalized barbarism protected by law, sanctioned by social mores, unquestioned by those who saw nothing wrong with buying and selling human flesh. Would that "peculiar institution" have ended without the "outrageous" and "illegal" actions of Quakers like William Lloyd Garrison and former slaves like Harriet Tubman and Sojourner Truth, men and women who were willing to spend their lives as social outlaws, to go to prison—and even die—to end slavery?

Philip was becoming increasingly impatient with people who thought that working within the system would end the war. To Philip it was clear that the way to end the war and build a new society was through nonviolent revolution, not polite reform. Attempting to explain his position to friends, Philip wrote that the war was not an effort to protect the Vietnamese from communism but, rather, a means to expand the U.S. empire. The Vietnam War was not a miscalculation but imperialism at work. Not noblesse oblige but genocide. The Vietnam War, Philip declared, was transatlantic schooners packed toe to toe with kidnapped Africans . . . women bleeding to death in the snow at Wounded Knee . . . tubercular children working sixteen-hour days in factories. Vietnam was who we'd always been, who we were, and who we'd always be, unless people decided to radically *trans*form, not just *re*form, the government, the church, themselves.

As they walked, Philip explained that he and a few friends were planning yet another action, venturing even deeper into nonviolent protest. Might Dan consider joining them, knowing that the price would be prison, further alienation from friends, rejection by some of the people they most loved? There could be no turning back now, said Philip. The war would go on and on until every Vietnamese village was smashed, every city burned, until *all* of the Vietnamese were dead. It no longer mattered whether people hated or loved the Berrigans. It didn't matter whether they would go to prison, whether the church censored, ignored, ridiculed them. What mattered was simply that they act in good faith, directly, with courage, to end the war.

On May 17, 1968, Daniel, Philip, and seven friends entered the draft board at Catonsville, Maryland, and walked directly to the file cabinets containing the names of young American males about to be called into the military. The nine dumped files into wire baskets and, followed by a distraught clerk yelling, "My files! my files!," carried them out. Another clerk threw a telephone through a window, hoping to attract attention. From their jail cells, the protesters would order that flowers and a note of apology be sent to the head clerk.

In the parking lot, the demonstrators poured homemade napalm (gasoline and soap chips concocted from formula in a Green Beret handbook) over the files, then struck a match. The files bubbled and burned. Cameras whirred, shutters snapped, sirens wailed, clerks wept, and the nine clasped hands, quietly praying. They did not run. No getaway cars or helicopter rescues, no chase scenes. The FBI raced to the scene. Cardinal Spellman, who would wear spit-shined paratrooper boots when he visited the troops in Vietnam, received a call—the Catholic Left had struck again. This time, praise God, they would surely go to jail for a long, very long time. The *New York Times* stated that 562 Americans and 5,000 Vietnamese had died the week before Catonsville.

Reaction to the Catonsville protest was resoundingly negative. Even some of those the Berrigans had counted on for support joined the chorus of denunciations—the action was "useless," "violent," "an assault on property," "scandalous."[5] But as the trial opened, supporters of the Catonsville Nine—nuns, priests, rabbis, ministers, students—stood in line each morning, jamming Judge Marion Thomsen's courtroom wall to wall. Vacillating between curiosity and his duty, as he defined it, to the law of the land, Judge Thomsen allowed the defendants to explain why they had taken such a dramatic, controversial, and "illegal" action to stop the war. He allowed the Nine to speak about their religious training, ethical beliefs, and the circuitous road that lead to Catonsville—odd, as he would later instruct the jury to ignore this testimony.

Describing how the church had exiled him to Baltimore for speaking out against the war, how he and others marched, wrote letters, petitioned, and met with government officials, Philip Berrigan concluded:

"I am saying merely this:

"We see no evidence that the institutions of this country, including our own churches, are able to provide the type of change that justice calls for, not only in this country, but around the world.

"We believe that this has occurred because law is no longer serving the needs of the people, which is a pretty good definition of morality."[6]

Thomas Melville, a priest, told the court how, like other idealistic priests and nuns in the 'fifties, he had gone to Central America to help the people. And how, just as Dan Berrigan had been transformed by the things he'd seen during his exile, the sight of so much unnecessary poverty changed his own views. In Guatemala, Melville explained, a tiny percentage of the people owned all of the land while the rest went hungry every day, watching their children die, living in a state of permanent hopelessness. And those who objected, who dared raise their voices to protest these inequities were "disappeared," their mutilated bodies (when they were found at all) a warning to others. All of this occurred, Melville continued, with the open support and approval of the U.S. government and the tacit support of the church. So disillusioned had Melville become that he had decided to join the Guatemalan revolutionary movement.

"You mean to say," asked the astonished judge, "that the United States government is executing Guatemalans?"

"Yes, your honor," Father Melville calmly answered.

When it was his turn to testify, Daniel Berrigan said to the court:

> *Our apologies good friends*
> *for the fracture of good order the burning of*
>     *paper*
> *instead of children the angering of the orderlies*
> *in the front parlor of the charnel house*
> *We could not so help us God do otherwise*
> *for we are sick at heart our hearts*
> *give us no rest for thinking of the Land of*
>     *Burning*
>
> *Children*[7]

When testimony concluded, Judge Thomsen complimented Daniel Berrigan on his eloquence, and informed the defendants they were getting exactly what they wanted. He then explained to the jury that they must rule only on whether Berrigan *et al.* had willingly destroyed government property. All else, said the judge, was inconsequential. On October 9, 1968, the jury found the defendants guilty as charged on each of three counts: destruction of U.S. government property, destruction of Selective Service records, and interference with the Selective Service Act of 1967. In November, all nine were sentenced to up to three years in federal prison and, with the exception of Phillip Berrigan and Tom Lewis, released on appeal. Philip and Tom had been sentenced to six years in prison for the Baltimore action, and a three-and-one-half-year concurrent term for Catonsville.

Daniel returned to Cornell where, as at universities and colleges throughout the United States, the war was opening chasms of misunderstanding and hatred between its supporters and opponents. In spring 1969, supporters of the war firebombed Cornell's Annabel Taylor Hall, the epitome of Ivy League grace and the command center for the anti-war movement. A short time later, black students armed with shotguns and rifles marched into Willard Straight Hall to protest racism and administrative indifference to blacks on campus. A year later, the Black Studies Building was burned. Threats and counterthreats ricocheted off the walls of Cornell's once-sedate stone buildings. Across the nation and in Southeast Asia the war was billowing out of control.

Richard Nixon's secret plan for ending the war turned out to be more bombing of the north and the mining of Haiphong Harbor, more killing in the southern half of Vietnam, and the invasion of Laos and Cambodia. At Kent State and Jackson State, young students were wounded and shot dead by the National Guard and police. In Chicago and Washington, D.C., the Weathermen called for the working class to rise up and overthrow the government, fought hand-to-hand battles with the "pigs," then went underground to organize revolution. Paid provocateurs infiltrated Vietnam Veterans Against the War (VVAW) and Students For A Democratic Society (SDS). Informers opened the mail and tape-recorded the lectures of anti-war professors. Anonymous sources leaked sordid tales of sex and violence in the peace movement to the press. FBI agents and city police scrambled to kill or imprison members of the Black Panther Party, ROTC buildings and banks were firebombed, and students plastered their dormitory and apartment walls with posters of Che Guevara, Mao Tse-tung, Huey Newton, and Fidel Castro. *Power from the barrel of a gun, not the petals of a flower. Off the pigs. Up against the wall.* . . . Martin Luther King, Jr. was dead, Gandhi passé, Philip and Daniel Berrigan on their way to the house of the dead, and "happiness is a warm gun."

As the date set for Dan and Phil's surrender to federal marshals approached, they weighed various arguments for and against going willingly to prison. After much soul-searching, during which they realized their refusal to submit would undoubtedly be misunderstood by their supporters, they decided to go underground. Within less than two weeks, FBI agents captured Philip at New York's St. Gregory's Church, where he'd gone to address an anti-war rally. But Dan eluded the FBI for four months, turning up at anti-war rallies, taping interviews for radio and television stations, disappearing just before his pursuers arrived. One evening, riding on the back of a motorcycle and disguised in helmet, goggles, and coveralls, Daniel Berrigan returned to Cornell's campus. Barton Hall was jammed with thousands of anti-war demonstrators who'd come to sing, chant, shout, and dance. A rock band was setting up on stage, watched closely by men in trench coats, aerials protruding above their collars. Dan walked onto the stage to foot-stomping and wall-shaking applause. He spoke briefly, explaining why he had decided to go underground rather than go willingly to prison. The lights dimmed and FBI agents scrambled, but it was too late. Wearing a huge papier-mache head of an apostle, Dan Berrigan joined the procession of Bread & Puppet players heading for the door. He was stuffed into the back of a van which raced, for the moment, out of the FBI's grasp.

"Well," Dan sighs, "it was a very interesting thing at Cornell when we got our date to actually turn ourselves in to federal marshals. And everybody was just in mourning about Berrigan." He laughs and shakes his head. "Oh, some people weren't in mourning at all. But, you know, we did have supporters in the religious community, among the chaplains and most of the faculty, and also a lot of students. And some people in the religious community organized a very beautiful farewell, and I knew all the while that I wasn't just going to surrender on the government's terms. So there was this great tearful farewell, and the university, under great protest from the students, played it very cannily, putting it in writing that I would be welcome back at Cornell. And I knew that I was going out the window at midnight.

"Well, I looked around that night and just felt very ambiguous. And when I reflected on it later it was very clear that the whole thing was ambiguous. Isn't that funny, clarity about ambiguity? In this sense: The people who were mourning my going to jail were appalled when I refused to submit, go quietly and docilely into prison. And some of them were furious, and remain so to this day. And isn't that interesting, said I to my soul. In other words, after every one of these—what shall I call actions like the Baltimore Four, Catonsville, the King of Prussia action—after these *breakthroughs*, there has always been a break*down*. You know, in the expectations of people about 'virtuous' conduct and what was to be done, and what was not to be done.

"So, of course, I went underground and managed to keep one step ahead of the FBI for several months, but that whole thing has been widely misunderstood. Because, you see, the real alternative to submitting to jail would have been to leave the country. I wasn't going to do that. And besides, all the time I was underground I was courting capture. I was doing that very deliberately, trying to raise the issue of the war in Vietnam. So my refusal to submit and my refusal to leave the country were, in my mind, both elements of responsibility. I couldn't just submit while that war was on, because that would be like being inducted into the war. That was the way I was thinking."

Daniel Berrigan would spend seventeen months, 575 days, in Danbury federal prison, where doctors shot Cortisone directly into the bone of his arthritic elbow, and his herniated esophagus, irritated by the prison diet of grease and starch, burned like an ulcer. He would fight against depression and despair, apathy and debilitating rage. One day an assistant preparing him for dental work accidentally pierced one of Dan's arteries. His breathing stopped, his lungs shut down, his heart wobbled. He lost consciousness. When he awoke, his brother Philip was by his side, crying.

Philip had been confined in Lewisburg, a tough maximum-security prison, where he and another Catonsville Nine member, David Eberhardt, were placed in solitary confinement. The men fasted, refusing to take anything but liquids for two weeks. Outside the prison, demonstrators rallied on their behalf. Harvard psychiatrist and author Robert Coles also paid Berrigan a visit and would later lobby to get Philip transferred to a less dangerous facility. "We talked to Coles about the oppression of the federal mentality," Philip would later write, "and the reactionary nature of local politics. Given time and a certain logic, our masters could as well convert this seat of misery into an extermination camp, and stoke the furnaces, convinced that they were serving God and man."[8]

Philip was transferred to Danbury, where he and Daniel struggled to understand and accept one another as brothers and friends. For a time, Philip was almost overwhelmed with envy and jealousy, imagining that Daniel held secret ambitions, that he was about to give in to his ego, sell out, become yet another "dimestore liberal," signing books at cocktail parties while Philip and others spent their days in solitary. Hurt and confused, Dan asked Philip to substantiate his accusations or drop them. Within this bizarre, Kafkaesque setting it would take discipline, even monumental effort, to think clearly, Dan warned. Indeed, as Dan and Philip would soon come to realize, prison officials were masters at turning Cain against Abel.

Philip recovered his perspective and he and Dan began working together, establishing a Great Books discussion club among inmates, writing and teaching about the war. Prison, they soon discovered, is designed to break the human spirit, to drive even hard-rock men and women to madness and despair. Minor infractions of the rules are severely punished, yet even in prison Dan and Phil continued their resistance activities, organizing a strike to protest against working conditions, filing a First Amendment suit on behalf of inmates who wanted to publish their writings in magazines and periodicals, defying all warnings and threats to end their antiwar activities.

On February 24, 1972, Daniel Berrigan stood in the snow

outside Danbury federal penitentiary. Reporters thrust microphones toward his chin, delighted supporters squeezed in for a closer look. In the background, snow stretched away to a line of trees and the concrete walls of the prison. The lines in his face were etched deeper, the mischievous eyes heavy-lidded, the smile somewhat tenuous, as though this might just be a practical joke. The war in Vietnam was still not over.

In Harrisburg, Pennsylvania, Philip was about to go on trial again, this time quite literally for his life. The charge: plotting to blow up heating ducts in the justice department and conspiring to kidnap Secretary of State Henry Kissinger. An indictment issued January 27, 1971, had listed Dan as an "unindicted co-conspirator," and later a "superseding" indictment charged Philip, Elizabeth McAlister, and others with conspiring to raid draft boards and obstruct the Selective Service System. The indictments did not explain how, confined to Danbury for nearly two years, the Berrigans might have accomplished these things.

In Danbury, Philip had befriended Boyd Douglas, an inmate who assured Berrigan that he too was opposed to the Vietnam War, that he too wanted to work for peace and social justice. Douglas was free to move in and out of the prison, and was trusted by other inmates for his willingness to carry contraband. Over a period of time, he had also developed the trust of anti-war activists. One day he offered to help Philip circumvent the censors, carrying Philip's letters out of prison, and letters from Elizabeth McAlister and other activists to Philip. What Douglas did not tell Philip or Elizabeth was that before giving their letters to friends and loved ones, he made photocopies for the FBI. Using these letters, and Douglas' extraordinary imagination, J. Edgar Hoover hoped to crush the Catholic Left and put the Berrigans away for good.

But if Hoover believed the Harrisburg trial would be the government's trump card, the bureau's ace in the hole, checkmate for the Pentagon, and the end of the line for the peace movement, he was mistaken. The war had gone on too long, draining the national treasury and the government's credibility. Hoover's grand tribunal turned out to be bad comedy, with the prosecution's star witness mugging truth or consequences for an unamused jury. For several days, Boyd Douglas, petty criminal and paid FBI informer, unraveled the darker figments of his imagination, bad plots for spy novels in which he believed he would surely be the star. The prosecutor read Philip and Elizabeth's private letters aloud, slowly, one by one, to the crowded courtroom. After deliberating longer than any jury in federal criminal history, jurors found Philip and Elizabeth guilty on only one count: passing contraband—their own private letters. Hoover's gambit had failed.

When the tumultuous 'sixties phased into the New Age 'seventies, Dan Berrigan did not sail away to the never-never shores of Esalen, start a dating service, or write a best-selling Jesuit cookbook. Philip didn't franchise encounter groups, star in freeze-dried nostalgia about the 'sixties, or vanish into the Himalayas, only to reappear as a Rolls Royce guru. After the fall of Saigon on April 30, 1975, Vietnam faded quickly into the folds of our collective amnesia and the arms race, though escalating day by day, was little more than a subliminal nag, something doom-and-gloomers brought up now and again on rather pleasant Sunday mornings. But why, when the church hierarchy banished him to Latin America, hadn't Daniel Berrigan just walked away, found some other way to wage the struggle for peace and social justice?

"Well," he replies, shaking his head and shrugging. "I don't know why. I guess I just didn't quit because that would have been a form of allowing that they were winning, that they had prevailed. Who knows, maybe there was something perverse in it but, I was not going to give up or give in."

In the courtroom, government prosecutors compared the hammers the Plowshare Eight used to "the tools of safe-crackers, bloodied knifes, guns," and Judge Samuel Salus III refused the defendants' request to call expert testimony from scientists, legal experts, Nobel Prize–winning scientists, and historians. Whether or not the world would survive, he insisted, was not the issue. Whether the Pentagon was really planning to attack the Soviet Union was not germane. Convinced there could be no dialogue or justice in the courtroom, the Berrigans and friends simply turned their backs on the judge, who later sentenced each defendant to from three to ten years in prison.

"Some who hear grow furious," Dan would later write. "Some of the furious are Catholics. Catholics also guard us, judge us, prosecute us. This is an old story, which need not long detain us.

"What is peculiar and of serious interest here is the use and misuse of symbols, their seizure by secular power; then the struggle to keep the symbols in focus, to enable them to be seen, heard, tasted, smelled, lived and died for, in all their integrity, first intent.

"Their misuse. How they are leveled off, made consistent

with the credo of the state. Thus, to speak of King of Prussia, and our symbol there: blood. Its outpouring in the death of Christ announced a gift and, by implication, set a strict boundary, a taboo. No shedding of blood, by anyone, under any circumstances, since 'this, My blood, is given for you.' Blood as a gift.

"Hence the command: No killing, no war, which is to say, above all, no nuclear weapons. And hence the imperative: Resist those who research, deploy, or justify, on whatever grounds such weaponry."[9]

"I mean," Dan explains, "when we did the Plowshares action in 1980, I could hear the church doors closing again all over the place, including these very liberal folk who had invited me to their pulpits, the big Protestant pulpits in the city. And when I said, 'Hey, what gives here? I've been preaching over there for years. Why, this gentleman whom I considered my friend wrote back a furious letter and it was the end of that. The end.

"You know, I've been through it all, the name-calling and great hatred coming at me, and now, getting to know the most amazing people—Anne Montgomery, Jean and Joe Gump, Lin Romano, Greg Boertje and so many others who are doing Plowshare actions. Catholics, religious sisters, all of that and everything in between, and the way I describe the changes taking place is that where there was once very great suspicion and hostility, and people turning their backs on us, there's now a lot of thoughtfulness. Not necessarily agreement, but there's questioning, a sense of the dislocation of something that looked very firm. You know, like 'We're number one in the world and war is great,' and all of that. And everywhere we go now, people come in amazing numbers. Oh, I don't mean whole stadiums full, but full halls to hear our story. And we very seldom encounter hostility. In fact, it's so rare that I may be too soft."

Dan laughs, closes his eyes for a moment.

"So, if there is hostility around, they don't come to hear me. I don't know," he says, with great modesty and more than a little incredulity. "There's some kind of disarming atmosphere around, among people, toward us. It's very concrete."

Daniel Berrigan and I walk around the corner from his apartment to a small Spanish restaurant where we order black bean soup topped with sour cream for lunch. The waiter is slow and surly, but Berrigan seems not to notice or to mind. And then we walk through the neighborhood, past small niches where the homeless build nests out of bits of urban flotsam and jetsam. Manhattan roars and swirls about us and we walk slowly, Dan pointing to a building that will soon be converted to expensive condominiums, driving more low income tenants into the streets. The city, Dan says, looks more and more like Calcutta.

We enter the subway, passing an emaciated woman and her small daughter begging for money. The woman extends a paper Coca-Cola cup, her jaundiced eyes beaming hatred and misery. I pass her quickly, as though trying not to get burned. As the subway screeches and rattles its way downtown, Dan explains that he is going to visit a young man who is dying of AIDS. The man's lover, says Berrigan, has patiently and steadfastly cared for his dying companion, using all of his energies and income to make him a little more comfortable, and to enable him to die with dignity. Dan is going, as he has so many times before for others, to hold the dying man's hand, listen, be a friend. He finishes the story and the subway reels around a sharp bend, halts in the station. We shake hands and, as he walks away, I think how odd he looks in his wrinkled pants, sneakers, and short-sleeve plaid shirt, like a retired merchant seaman on his way to the Blarney Rose for another lonely afternoon of double shots and cheering for the Mets.

Six times nominated for the Nobel peace prize with his brother Philip, recipient of the Lamont Poetry Award, three-time National Book Award nominee, Dan Berrigan is a legend in some parts of the world. During our brief visit, Dan had mentioned none of these things. No names dropped. No rhetorical flourishes or *I told you so*s. The subway pulls out of the station and I feel simultaneously happy and sad, inspired by the morning I've spent with Father Berrigan, depressed by what may be in store for him and the Plowshare Eight when their appeal runs out.

"Some kind of disarming atmosphere," said Berrigan, shaking his head and smiling. For which, I think as the train lurches into darkness, he just might die in prison.

# Notes

1. Thomas Merton, *Raids On The Unspeakable* (New York: New Directions, 1964), 54–55.

2. Allen and Linda Kirschner, *Blessed Are the Peacemakers* (New York: Popular Library, 1971), 226.

3. Daniel Berrigan, *Night Flight To Hanoi: War Diary with 11 Poems* (New York: Harper & Row, 1968), 113–114.

4. Albert Camus, *The Unbeliever And The Christian,* from Daniel Berrigan, *The Trial of the Catonsville Nine* (Boston: Beacon Press, 1970), 118.

5. Daniel Berrigan, *To Dwell In Peace* (New York: Harper & Row, 1987), 219.

6. Daniel Berrigan, *The Trial of the Catonsville Nine* (Boston: Beacon Press, 1970), 118.

7. Ibid., 60.

8. Philip Berrigan, *Widen the Prison Gates* (New York: Simon & Schuster, 1973), 47.

9. Arthur J. Laffin and Anne Montgomery, *Swords Into Plowshares* (New York: Harper & Row, 1987), 59.

# Three

## Prison Gates and Golden Pond: The Story of Jean and Joe Gump

> As for adopting the ways which the state has provided for remedying the evil, I know not of such ways.
> HENRY DAVID THOREAU

At the federal penitentiary for women in Alderson, West Virginia, the inmates are preparing for bed. Counted. Sorted like cards. Directed like children on the first day of summer camp. Sometime during this lazy West Virginia night, one of them will awake screaming. She is young, Puerto Rican, terrified at the silence in which she is enveloped. Her arms are thin, bruised, tiny pockmarks mapping the veins from wrist to elbow. Her heart pounds but she is in solitary, a box, a cave, a black hole from which no sound emerges. She lies awake, staring into the darkness that could be death, but isn't.

If she ever woke in the night crying, Plowshare activist Jean Gump doesn't do so now. Indeed, she tells visitors, she sleeps well enough and her appetite is good. She has already spent more than four years in prison for refusing to pay a $428.48 fine, and for refusing to sign an agreement promising not to engage in acts of civil disobedience. One day soon the gates will open and Jean will be allowed to leave Alderson, at least temporarily. The fine will still be pending, the pen and paper lying on the probation officer's desk. On July 12, 1987, Jean sent a letter to Joseph M. Brandenburg, Jr., Supervising U.S. Probation Officer, to explain that she would neither sign an agreement, nor pay the fine.

"Dear Mr. Brandenburg," Jean wrote, "Thank you for your prompt reply to my inquiry. As I glean from reading your letter, it seems that after serving the 6 years I will still be responsible to pay the $424.48 repair of the nuclear missile plus the $100.00 assessment.

"Could you ask Judge Hunter if rather than bringing me back into court for a probation violation—again not paying for the missile repair (which I won't) that he just add the 5 year probation time on to my sentence. That way the tax payers will be saved the cost of another trial. If he is able to do this I will serve 11 years. I would be eligible to rejoin my family in 1998. Now my question is this: will I still owe the government $424.48? Is there any other legal way, other than violating my conscience, in our system of justice to retire this debt? I sure hope so because I will be in prison a long long time.

"This is just an aside and you don't have to read it if you don't want to. I had read somewhere that it costs the taxpayers $28,000 per year per inmate for incarceration. Now, if my arithmetic is correct my confinement will cost $308,000. Maybe the government should pay the $424.48

and save themselves $307,475.52 for my continued incarceration."

Jean Gump's sentence, and that of other Plowshare activists—Helen Woodson, eighteen years; Carl Kabat, eighteen years; Paul Kabat, ten years; Daniel and Philip Berrigan, three to ten years—may seem unduly harsh. In many cases, rapists and murderers have gotten off much easier; however, it is not uncommon for Americans to serve time in prison for their opposition to or refusal to serve in war. For example, in June 1917, Congress passed the Espionage Act, making it a crime to criticize U.S. involvement in World War I. Under the provisions of this act, the government had the right to censor newspapers, ban certain publications from the mails, and jail anyone who "interfered" with the draft or enlistment of soldiers. Punishment for violating the Espionage Act was a maximum of twenty years in prison. Fired by patriotism, some states also passed laws limiting the rights of Americans to free speech and assembly.

Government agents raided labor halls, mostly those belonging to the International Workers of the World, or Wobblies, arresting many IWW leaders. Anarchists Emma Goldman and Alexander Berkman formed a No-Conscription League to "resist conscription by every means in our power" and were arrested in June 1917, charged with obstructing the draft, and sentenced to two years in prison plus a ten-thousand-dollar fine each. Socialist Kate Richards O'Hare was given five years in jail for an anti-war speech she made in North Dakota. Rose Pastor Stokes was sent to prison for ten years for writing a letter to the *Kansas City Star* accusing the government of favoring "profiteers" over people. Five members of the executive committee of the Socialist

Party were sentenced to twenty years in prison, and later the presiding judge said he regretted not being able to line Victor Berger, one of the defendants, up against a wall so he could be shot. Pacifists were beaten, forced to parade with ropes around their necks, threatened with execution, and sent to prison. A twenty-year-old woman received a fifteen-year prison sentence for distributing leaflets condemning Allied intervention in Russia. Eugene Debs was sentenced to ten years in prison for speaking out against the Espionage Act, was nominated for president by the Socialist Party, and won nearly a million votes while still in prison.

There are no bars on the visiting room's windows at Alderson, not even heavy screen, and watching the inmates stroll between buildings one almost expects to hear church bells, or see carloads of young men in Ivy League sweatshirts stopping to ask if a coed wants a ride to class. The prison's buildings are named after strong, articulate, free-spirited women like Susan B. Anthony and Barbara Jordan. There is no Angela Davis dining hill, Emma Goldman library, or Elizabeth McAlister visitor's center.

At her trial for entering a Minuteman II missile site at Whiteman Air Force Base near Warrensberg, Missouri, and pounding on a concrete missile silo cover with a hammer, Jean tried to tell Elmo B. Hunter, the presiding federal judge, about the years she had spent working within the system, believing that one day her elected officials would stop supporting the arms race. "I'm a law-and-order nut," Jean would later tell reporters. "When the speed limit says 25, that's what I go, not 26, not 30. My children don't even like to ride with me, because I obey the signs, even if it's 3:00 A.M. in the morning and there's not a car around." She had not wanted, Jean told the judge, to break the law, had not wanted to leave her husband and twelve children, and certainly did not want to spend years in prison. Nevertheless, she told Judge Hunter: "These laws that protect weapons are immoral, against international law, and simply must be broken. These are not laws that will contribute to life, but are protecting the end of our species, the destruction of our planet, because all of these laws are in place to protect nuclear weapons, not people. Our laws are designed, written, and enforced to protect the war industries. So they just have to be broken, and you may do what you have to do. I've already done what my conscience told me to."

Including its lunch break, the jury was out only an hour and thirty-nine minutes before finding Jean Gump, 59; Ken B. Rippeto, 21; Darla J. Bradley, 22; Lawrence A Morlan, 26; and John A. Volpe, 39, guilty of conspiracy and destroying government property. Judge Hunter called the defendants "arrogant," then sentenced all but John Volpe to eight years in prison. Because Volpe had three small children, Judge Hunter reduced his sentence to seven years in prison.

Jean Gump grew up in Chicago, an Irish Catholic but somewhat of an anomaly because her father was a Republican in a city controlled by the Democratic machine. She attended a girl's parochial high school, learning the importance of being Catholic and the necessity, if one were interested in succeeding, of belonging to the "right" party. In Jean's family conversation was an art form, the topic of discussion nearly always about who was about to run for or be thrown out of office. Sometimes tempers flared and an argument begun on Sunday might roll over into Monday, but rarely did anyone harbor hard feelings. It was all just part of the Irish passion for a rough-and-tumble game called politics.

One day a friend asked Jean if she might be interested in meeting a "cute fellow," and she said yes, assuming, since the only people she knew were Irish and Catholic, that the blind date would be straight from County Claire. But the young man turned out to be a handsome and charming German-American, so attractive that on their first date Jean looked at Joe Gump and said, "You know, buddy, some day I'm gonna marry you." As the date for their marriage approached, Jean was forced to reexamine her own prejudices and fears. Even though she had never had a German neighbor or friend, she knew that she hated *them*. She knew that *they* killed millions of Jews? *They* had started two World Wars? *They* were all racists? She hated *them*, but she was in love with Joe Gump and his family. How could this be? After much thought, Jean concluded that she was in fact one of *them*. She was capable of hating other people, blindly, totally, without even knowing those whom she despised. Though she had never murdered anyone with her hand, she certainly had with her heart. Hatred, she concluded, is not merely an irrational feeling or thought; hatred leads to war, killing, mass murder.

World War II had ended, and Jean and Joe were married in the afterglow of victory over Germany and Japan. They did not really understand why the U.S. had destroyed Hiroshima and Nagasaki. According to news accounts, dropping the atom bomb on these cities saved hundreds of thousands, perhaps even a million Allied troops. Moreover, with the secret of how to build the world's most powerful weapon known only to the U.S., world peace would be easier to maintain. But soon there were new rumors of war, almost-daily warnings that the "free world" was facing an even greater threat than Nazism. The year before Joe and Jean were married, President Truman had dispatched atomic-capable B-29s to bases in Britain and Germany in response to the blockade of Berlin. Shortly after their honeymoon, the Soviet Union tested an atomic weapon six times more powerful than the bomb that killed 100,000 people in Hiroshima. U.S. scientists then began working on a "super bomb" that would have the explosive yield of 50 to 1750 Hiroshima bombs. Schoolchildren, some of whom had been born on the day U.S. and Soviet troops were embracing on the banks of the Elbe River in Germany, were shown films and read books about the evils of Communism. In the middle of a recitation, teachers would cry "Duck and Cover!" and children would scramble beneath their desks to wait out a mock atomic attack. The catechism of the Cold War had begun.

Joe completed his degree at the Illinois Institute of Technology and the Gumps began having their twelve children. He was a chemical engineer, hard-driving, dedicated, upwardly mobile. Later, Jean would joke that she had the longest pregnancy on the block—fourteen years. They were devout Catholics, naming the rooms in their suburban home after the saints, rousing the children on Sunday morning and, once cereal bowls were collected, and the spilled milk and sugar sponged clean, heading off to St. Martha's Church. In suburban communities, sprinklers twirled through lazy afternoons, creating rainbows through which children leapt and danced. On weekends, cars and tricycles were parked wheel to wheel in driveways, lawnmowers hummed like locusts, and neighbors gathered, bowls of popcorn and bottles of beer in hand, to watch a strange and wonderful new invention called television. The sweet-and-sour pall of charcoal smoke floated from block to block like prosperity.

Yet just beneath this tranquil surface were contradictions

that, long before the tumultuous 'sixties, had begun to shift like tectonic plates. A short distance from the powder rooms and manicured lawns of suburban Chicago, street gangs fought hand to hand over "turf," killing one another for control of a two-block stretch of rat-infested tenements. In the South signs above water fountains and toilets declared WHITES ONLY, while in the North real estate brokers smiled when the caller was white, said "no vacancy" when the prospective buyer was black or Hispanic.

To many, if not most, Catholics, discrimination was simply a fact of life, something no one ever could, or should, change. To Joe and Jean Gump, racism was a form of blasphemy, totally inconsistent with the teachings of Christ. Most of their fellow Americans believed that people were poor because they were lazy, inept, or stupid. The Gumps insisted that poverty, like wealth, is inherited, the result of social inequalities rather than human defects.

In the late 'fifties, the Gumps joined the Christian Family Movement, the motto of which was to: "Observe, Judge, and Act." At a conference held on Notre Dame's campus, they met two handsome and charismatic brothers, one a Josephite priest, the other a Jesuit. The priests were soft-spoken, yet extraordinarily compelling in their argument that in a world so filled with poverty, racism, and injustice, a Christian must not be passive. They made no firebrand speeches, no attempts to persuade their listeners to commit civil disobedience. Yet hearing Philip and Daniel Berrigan for the first time was a profound experience for the Gumps, an inspiring relief from the file-drawer homilies on the evils of Communism or the sacred duty of Catholics to obey God *and* country.

Before joining the Christian Family Movement, Joe and Jean had assumed that only priests could get involved in peace-and-justice issues. Priests could take a stand on war and peace, speak out on racism, work to end hunger and injustice. Through their involvement with CFM, the Gumps began to discover a new vision of what it meant to be a Christian. They had no way of knowing at the time the degree to which this vision would instruct their lives, or the price—estrangement from friends, ridicule, and years in prison—they would pay for their beliefs.

One afternoon, Jean and her four-year-old son Joey were watching television when the film *Judgment at Nuremberg* was abruptly interrupted by scenes of men and women walking toward a bridge in Selma, Alabama. A man with a bullhorn was warning them to turn back, and suddenly policemen on horseback were riding into the crowd, lashing out with bullwhips, pounding demonstrators to the ground with long clubs, trampling nuns and priests who were walking at the front of the group. Joey watched the attack with a kind of dreamy curiosity, turning to his mother, then watching, turning, watching. Jean listened to the sounds of clubs falling, horses snorting, screams, sirens, the soft *pop-pop-pop* of tear-gas canisters fired into the ranks of the demonstrators.

"Mommy?" the boy asked, pointing to the screen.

"Yes, Joey?" Jean's eyes were filling with tears of frustration and anger. "What are you going to do about that, Mommy?"

A commercial break. Jean was stunned. What right did he have to say that to her? The boy waited. But, Jean thought, hadn't she always told her children that when they saw an injustice, they must not to wait for someone else to do something about it. "Don't just stand there," she had said. "Observe. Judge. Act."

"Well?" the boy persisted, his nose inches from Jean's face, "Well, Mommy?"

Suddenly she realized that he was just repeating her own words. Her son had taken her advice, quite literally. What *was* she going to do about it? Could she back off now, after what she had been telling her children for so many years? Could she pretend that racism, violence, and social injustice were someone else's problem?

Jean knew the risks of going to Alabama: Jimmy Lee Jackson, a young black man, had been beaten and fatally shot by state troopers when he tried to keep them from attacking his mother. Richard Valeriani, a newsman, was nearly killed by segregationists who hit him in the head with an axe handle. The Rev. James Reeb had died after being knocked unconscious by club-wielding racists. And even now, on Alabama's backroads and highways, Klansmen were waiting to ambush and kill the "nigger-loving" interlopers from the North.

Jean told her family and friends that she was going to Alabama, and was surprised when a CFM member demanded to know what right a mother of twelve children had to be risking her life. "Observe. Judge. Act," Jean Gump replied. Joe agreed to baby-sit for a few days and Jean boarded a Greyhound bus in the middle of the night with other civil rights activists.

In 1964, Congress passed the Civil Rights Act, and a year later the historic Voting Rights Act, but discrimination and violence continued, in both the South and the North. On April 4, 1967, Martin Luther King, Jr., delivered one of his most dramatic and controversial speeches before a gathering in New York City's Riverside Church, arguing that it was absurd and hypocritical to send young black men to fight for liberties in Southeast Asia that they did not yet enjoy in their own country. Jean Gump read excerpts from King's speech, and the numerous editorials warning that he had gone beyond the domain of civil rights, swung to the left, and joined the extremists. Editorials, she thought, that read like death sentences.

Jean continued to march, sing, and write letters to her congressmen, lobbying against a war in which one of her brothers fought, while another brother went to Canada. At St. Martha's, the fighting and dying in Southeast Asia seemed merely a time-warped version of World War II. The sides were clear-cut, the goals noble, and the war's opponents traitors. Jean's brother returned from Vietnam, sold his gun collection, stopped hunting and, like most combat veterans, refused to talk about his tour of duty.

FBI agents often cruised the streets of Jean's neighborhood, or waited outside the Gump's house, hoping to arrest the brother who had burned his draft card. Sometimes they came to the door, asking if the Gumps could tell them how to find Jean's brother. One afternoon they knocked on the door and Jean invited them into the living room, politely but firmly ordering them to sit down. "Now listen here," she shouted, "the Mafia is running the city of Chicago. Crime is totally out of control. And you, you're out looking for *my* brother. Why don't you go out and do something important instead of wasting the taxpayers' money looking for pacifists who aren't hurting anybody?"

"In other words, you won't cooperate?" the agents asked.

"That's right," Jean replied. "You got that real, real good."

In the summer of 1972, a friend asked Jean if she might

be interested in being a delegate to the Democratic National Convention. She quickly agreed, was approved by the screening committee, ran as an alternate, and won. George McGovern might not win, she told friends, but at least he offered a real alternative to the coalition of white-collar criminals and right-wing ideologues who were running the nation. Before she left for Miami, Jean attended a conference of delegates in Springfield, Illinois. As the delegates sat about idly talking and smoking, a crier announced the "Honorable Mayor of Chicago, Richard Daley." Everyone leaped to their feet, while Jean remained seated. "His Honor is a racist," she explained to the astonished delegates, "and I don't stand up for people like that." Later, Jean found the Democratic convention deeply disappointing. The hard-working, idealistic delegates she'd expected to find turned out to be more interested in getting drunk than developing a platform, more concerned with how they might appear on television than challenging the rules committee.

Jean Gump left Miami discouraged and disillusioned. In one quick and painful lesson she had discovered how little she really knew about politics. She had gone to the convention with a serious purpose, believing that the Democratic Party would develop a meaningful platform: a guaranteed income for every American, an end to poverty, and an end to the fighting in Vietnam. But after several days of shouting and singing, rhetoric and bombast, boasting and bravado, the only real result was the nomination of a presidential candidate who had no chance of winning in the November elections.

Richard Nixon was re-elected and the war continued. Secretary of State Henry Kissinger threatened the North Vietnamese with atomic weapons unless they capitulated to U.S.

demands, and they refused. Saigon fell and the nation slumbered, numbed by its losses and years of internecine quarreling. Abbie Hoffman was arrested for possession of cocaine and vanished. Jerry Rubin started a dating service. The Symbionese Liberation Army kidnapped Patty Hearst and called for the working class to destroy "the insects that prey upon the people." Many of their members died when the police set fire to the house in which they were hiding. Ronald Reagan watched and waited, defeated Jimmy Carter for the presidency, and promised "peace through strength." Jean Gump continued her efforts to work within the system for political and social change.

Jean joined the movement to freeze the arms race, believing that if people were educated to the truth, then surely they would act on it. Members of her group invited experts to speak on the effects of the arms race on children, the economy, and the environment. They showed films like *Gods of Metal* and *Atomic Cafe*, conducted surveys, and sponsored forums, colloquiums, and debates. They visited secondary schools, developed educational materials, and invited politicians, government officials, and military officers to defend their positions on new weapons systems. On June 12, 1982, more than a million people marched through the streets of Manhattan to demand that the Soviet Union and United States stop the development, deployment, and testing of atomic weapons. The arms race continued.

Jean grew impatient with the gradualist approach to ending the arms race, convinced that she and others in the Freeze Movement were merely marking time, preaching to the converted, playing at a game whose rules they did not understand. The real problem was not whether the world could survive a nuclear war. Even if that were possible, who would want to crawl about a moonscape where hundreds of millions of bodies lay bloated and unburied, the sun was obscured by dust and smoke, and the best parents could hope for would be to watch their children die agonizingly slowly, their hair falling out in clumps, vomiting their own intestines? Everyone had heard these scenarios and, when the speaker finished or the lights were turned on after a particularly gruesome film, people would just sit around sipping tea and nibbling cookies, dropping crumbs and maybe an occasional tear on the postcards they were sending to their congressperson or Ronald Reagan.

The real problem wasn't convincing people they would die in a nuclear war, or from the effects of radiation and nuclear winter that would ensue. Anyone with a modicum of good sense knew that. The problem was telling people that our country—that dapper, educated, silver-tongued fellow who always danced the foxtrot at family parties; that gracious, kindhearted, generous churchgoer who delivered turkeys to the poor on Thanksgiving and rang the Salvation Army bell at Christmas; that bastion of virtue we all trusted and loved with such devoted filial passion—is a hit-man, mercenary, manipulator, swindler, split personality, genius of disguise, black belt in sleight of hand, world-class conjurer.

The deeper Jean Gump looked into the history of the arms race, the more apparent it became that nearly everything she'd heard or read about it was untrue. If atomic weapons were strictly for defensive purposes, then why had every president from Harry Truman to Ronald Reagan—with the possible exception of Gerald Ford—either pondered the use of, or actually directed preparations for, a U.S. atomic strike somewhere the world? Why, she wondered, hadn't her own children learned in school that shortly after the U.S. Marines were surrounded by Communist troops at the Chosin Reservoir in Korea, the U.S. threatened to use atomic weapons against the Chinese? Why had she never known that the U.S. offered to give the French tactical nuclear weapons in 1954 to save their garrison at Dien Bien Phu, and that Jimmy Carter, an ardent Christian, made nuclear weapons an integral part of his Middle East Doctrine?

Why all the fictions about "missile gaps" and "windows of vulnerability," when from the beginning of the arms race the U.S. was far ahead of the Soviet Union in developing new weapons systems? Why had our government refused to agree to a "no first use" of nuclear weapons when the Soviet Union had repeatedly indicated its desire to do so bilaterally? Why had we refused to agree to a freeze on the testing and deployment of new weapons systems, when our adversary had suggested such a possibility on more than one occasion?

The American people, Jean discovered, had been lied to by the government about the dangers of low-level radiation. Soldiers witnessing atomic tests in Nevada had been told that the risks were minuscule. People living downwind from atomic test sites were told they were in little danger of exposure to cancer-causing radiation. Residents of the Bikini atoll had been deceived about the dangers of radioactivity in their soil and food supplies. Scientists whose studies suggested high-risk correlations between radiation exposure and cancer were fired, blacklisted, denied research grants.

Certainly her friends in the Freeze Movement were well-meaning, deeply caring people. Like men and women everywhere they just wanted their children to grow up in a world free of the threat of nuclear annihilation. They wanted their government and the Soviet Union to stop squandering hundreds of billions of dollars that could be spent to feed the hungry, house the poor, clean up the world's poisoned environment. Billions that could be spent on cultural exchanges and art exhibits, music fairs and sports tournaments, puppet shows and scholarships, environmental think tanks where human genius could be put to work to find new ways to prolong, not destroy, life on earth.

Her friends were hard-working, concerned, idealistic, but wasn't writing polite editorials to newspapers, sending postcards to congressmen, and showing films to the already persuaded like asking the executioner for a loan as he was about to raise the guillotine? Besides, the arms race was not an anomaly, something odd and slightly unsavory in an otherwise unblemished democracy. Like Daniel and Philip Berrigan and other members of the Catholic Left, Jean had concluded that the arms race is as American as the Mafia, slavery, Indian massacres, and robber barons. The arms race is really a measure of how much we believe in violent solutions to interpersonal and international disagreements. In a suicidal culture, Jean Gump would tell astonished friends, the arms race is merely the primary method we've chosen to kill ourselves.

Along with members of the Disarm Now Action Group, and later with the Chicago Life Community, Jean began getting arrested, hoping that civil disobedience would make some difference. Members of the CLC also attended the annual stockholders' meetings at Morton Thiokol—the company that manufactures all the solid rocket fuel for missiles. Dressed in suits and stockings, their hair brushed into the latest style, Jean and friends would disrupt the meetings by handing out leaflets and trying to open a dialogue with the stockholders who were all women, Jean's age or older. "Do you know what you are doing? I mean, using the profits from your own company to destroy the world?" Jean would demand.

"Well," they would answer, "If we don't do it somebody else will." Mr. Morton-Thiokol never did accept their invitation to exchange views on the arms race.

*Acceptable losses. Limited nuclear warfare. Protracted nuclear war. Surgical strike. Decapitating Strike. Strategic nuclear forces. The U.S. must be able to wage nuclear war "rationally." The U.S. should develop an intelligent offensive strategy. The U.S. must be prepared to sustain acceptable losses. Nuclear war can be won.*

Reading such things in the early 'eighties, not in supermarket tabloids but respectable newspapers, made Jean's temples throb and her hackles rise in anger. No mention of the mountainous funeral pyres. No reference to disintegrating playgrounds, cremated nursery schools, families out on a Sunday stroll instantly vaporized, churches and hospitals and schools and playing fields and art galleries and universities and synagogues turned to ash. This was bloodless language, spun from computer onto paper where it lay like last November's leaves—soggy, meaningless, dead. Yet she knew that most of the people who wrote about such things got out of bed on Sundays and, just as she and Joe did, drove off to church with their families. Just like Joe and her, they sang about the birth and death of Christ, prayed for justice, asked for God's mercy. Had the arms race driven the authors of such articles to some radical bifurcation between spirit and intellect, morality and political expediency? Were the proponents of these doomsday scenarios insane?

Thomas Merton had also wondered about such things, but after much thought had concluded that on the contrary:

It is the sane ones, the well-adapted ones, who can without qualms and without nausea aim the missiles and press the buttons that will initiate the great festival of destruction that they, *the sane ones,* have prepared. . . . No one suspects the sane, and the sane ones will have *perfectly good reasons,* logical, well-adjusted reasons, for firing the first shot. . . .

Perhaps what is needed, Merton concluded, is a new definition of sanity in the nuclear age: "We can no longer assume that because a man is 'sane' he is therefore in his 'right mind.' The whole concept of sanity in a society where spiritual values have lost their meaning is itself meaningless. A man can be 'sane' in the limited sense that he is not impeded by his disordered emotions from acting in a cool, orderly, manner, according to the needs and dictates of the social situation in which he finds himself. He can be perfectly 'adjusted.' God knows, perhaps such people can be perfectly adjusted even in hell itself."[2]

How curious, Jean thought, that local parishes continued to avoid confronting the issue of nuclear war directly and with courage, that the church's hierarchy had failed to offer real hope to hundreds of millions of people living in despair and fear. Surely American parish priests, bishops, and archbishops had read Pope John XXIII's *Pacem in Terris,* in which the Holy Father said, clearly and without equivocation:

Justice, then right reason and humanity urgently demand that the arms race should cease. That the stockpiles which exist in various countries should be reduced equally and simultaneously by the parties concerned. That nuclear weapons should be banned. And that a general agreement should eventually be reached about progressive disarmament and an effective method of control. In the words of Pius XII, our predecessor of happy memory: "The calamity of a world war, with the economic and social ruin and the moral excesses and dissolution that accompany it, must not be permitted to envelop the human race for a third time."[3]

Yet somehow this message failed to reach many of the clergy, or, if it did, was carefully filtered through several decades of Cold War rhetoric. In July 1981, the National Conference of Catholic Bishops authorized a committee of five U.S. bishops, chaired by Joseph Bernardin, Archbishop of Chicago, to draft a pastoral letter on the subject of nuclear war. The committee prepared three drafts, and, after spirited debate, released the 150-page document, *The Challenge of Peace: God's Promise and Our Response*, to the public. Earlier drafts were made available to the press and government representatives, and the Reagan administration reacted quickly, challenging the anti-war tone of the second draft. After talking over these challenges, and consulting with European church officials, the bishops revised their letter, making their opposition to nuclear war less categorical. For example, they said, a Soviet attack on NATO forces might justify a nuclear response by the United States. The bishops wrote:

> We see with clarity the political folly of a system which threatens mutual suicide; the psychological damage this does to ordinary people, especially the young; the economic distortion of priorities—billions readily spent

for destructive instruments and pitched battles being waged daily in our legislatures about a fraction of this amount for the homeless, the hungry and the helpless here and abroad. We see with much less clarity how we translate a "no" to nuclear war into the personal and public choices which can move us in a new direction, toward a national policy and an international system which more adequately reflect the values and vision of the Kingdom of God. . . .

The political paradox of deterrence has also strained our moral conception. May a nation threaten what it may never do? May it possess what it may never use? Who is involved in the threat each superpower makes: government officials? or military personnel? or the citizenry in whose "defense" the threat is made?[4]

About nonviolent civil disobedient resistance to the arms race, the bishops concluded:

Non-violent resistance requires the united will of a people and may demand patience and suffering from those who practice it. It may not always succeed. But before the possibility is dismissed as impractical or unrealistic we urge that it be measured against the almost certain effects of a major war. . . .[5]

In the days before the action at Whitman Air Force base, Jean's husband had watched and wondered. Jean Gump never lied. This much he knew beyond question. She and Joe had always talked things out, sometimes disagreeing, Jean always the pacesetter, the Christian existentialist, curious, querulous, occasionally downright quarrelsome, always committed. *Observe. Judge. Act.* But now he watched her disappear into weekend retreats from which she returned, if not transformed then changed, more introspective, walking through the house as though the floors were made of thin ice.

She could not tell her family: *Sell your things, say goodbye to your family. Don't look back, come, follow me.* That's what Christ had said. Not, "Oh well, put your things in storage for awhile, invest in a few CDs, have a knockdown drag-out or two with your boss and family, then call me if things work out. We'll run through the pros and cons of letting go." No, He said, quite simply, *Follow Me.* For Jean and the friends with whom she'd been meeting for the past year, this could mean long years in prison, even death. At the very least, an end to an era. The right thing, she would tell friends, family, journalists, "for me at the time."

Three things, Jean Gump believes, are impediments to truth: family, possessions, and self. In her den was a chair, worn with sitting and furrowed to the contours of her body, changing year after year to accommodate pounds gained or lost. In the kitchen, her Mixmaster, the blades smooth as soapstone, bowls winking happily, washed, dried, set in their place after a thousand cakes, pies, and cookies; after births, weddings, anniversaries, baptisms. And her grandmother's crystal sugar bowl, a small shrine to memory. All the talismans holding her down with their magic. She understood how, facing floods, hurricanes, Gestapo round-ups, human beings often cling to their possessions, believing that somehow their heirlooms and antiques, houses and jewels, will make them invincible.

Good Friday, 1986. The car's heater hummed. Jean looked out the window but the land was cast in shadow, somewhere between night and day. Out there, as though seeded by some diabolical giant, is the end of the world: huge, carefully concealed concrete lids tucked neatly into the rolling hills and set to roll back on iron tracks, releasing a fifty-seven-foot-long, thirty-six-ton missile to soar over corn and wheat, barns and houses, schools and milk cows.

The nausea was gone. Thoughts of bullets smashing into bone, gone. Images of a casket, banks of flowers, an organ dirge, her children and Joe sobbing, gone. A good day to die, Native American warriors cried as they rode out to meet the cavalry. Jean did not wish to die, but it hardly mattered now.

Jean Gump and Larry Morlan, a twenty-five-year-old former seminarian who was working and living among the poor in a *Catholic Worker* house, draped a SWORDS INTO PLOW-SHARES banner over the fence surrounding the Minuteman II silo. Ken Rippeto, *Catholic Worker* activist and former seminarian, was cutting through the fence with bolt-cutters, and the protesters squeezed through. Larry pounded on electrical outlets, chiseled a cross into the maintenance hatch. Jean poured blood, her own, from baby bottles onto the concrete, forming a near perfect cross. When the bottles were empty, she spraypainted DISARM AND LIVE on the missile's concrete cover. She clipped through sensor wires, and miraculously was not electrocuted.

At another silo, Darla Bradley, a young woman who grew up on an Iowa farm and decided to dedicate her life to working with the poor, and John Volpe, former history teacher, father of three children and a *Catholic Worker* activist, were also pounding on concrete, pouring their own blood, spraypainting. After about twenty minutes, Jean, Ken, and Larry sat down and began singing. Beneath them, they heard the hum of the missile's air conditioning system and then, outside the fence, a slightly scolding, condescendingly familiar voice:

> *Mike Wallace:* Do you really believe that this puny manifestation . . . is going to make any difference whatsoever?
>
> *Ken:* The difference is that we created a symbol to show that disarmament will happen one dent at a time.
>
> *Wallace:* Are you aware that what you're doing this morning could conceivably put you behind bars for some time?
>
> *Jean:* Small price to pay. It isn't what we want to do.
>
> *Wallace:* Don't we need defense? Our government would say that this proves we are strong. Therefore, it would deter someone else from trying to attack us. They would call it an instrument of peace.
>
> *Jean:* These are not peacekeepers. The government only wants more power, more death capabilities. We're all hostages. I don't want to be that anymore. Enough is enough.

An armored personnel carrier arrived, a machine-gunner in the turret, the vehicle itself seeming to talk, ordering all personnel on top of that silo to leave the premises "with your hands up." A soldier leapt from the vehicle and knelt with his M-16 pointing at Jean's head. Another, also in full battle dress, stood with an automatic rifle aimed at the protesters. Jean and the men crawled through the hole in the fence and stood with hands raised, the men spread-eagled against the wire, patted down, frisked. Jean's arms began to tingle and ache, the circulation in her hands shutting down. "*No!*" her young guard cried when she slowly lowered her arms, "*Put your hands up!*"

Jean tried to explain that she was losing circulation in her hands, but the boy was nervous, frightened, unsure if his prisoner was a cunning terrorist or someone's deranged grandmother.

"Okay," Jean said, trying to calm her captor. "How about if we reach a compromise? I'll put my hands up for awhile, and then when the circulation stops again, I'll put them down."

The boy's eyes widened and he took a step backward, closer to the armored carrier. "*No!*" he repeated. "You can't do that!"

Jean smiled, imagining him seated at her dining room table, the turkey steaming, cranberries glistening in her favorite crystal dish, mashed potatoes, candied yams, everyone holding hands, eyes closed. "Thank you God for this food, this home, this life, love, peace . . ."

"I'm gonna do it," she said.

"You can't."

"Then shoot me."

The boy looked confused, and angry, but did not fire.

Inside the armored car, Jean noticed a large sign: PEACE KEEPER. "My God," she called to the soldier standing outside, his M-16 pointing at her nose. "They call this a peacekeeper? This is not a peacekeeper, this is a *warkeeper*." The soldier did not respond. "Hey," Jean persisted, "Did you ever by chance read George Orwell's *1984*?"

"Well, yes, Ma'am," the soldier replied, glancing nervously about. "But I just can't talk to you about that now."

"Well, I'm going to talk to *you* about it."

A long pause, and the guard moved his rifle to the right, and bent slightly at the waist.

"Well, someday when I'm not in uniform we should sit and have coffee."

"That's a good idea. I would really like that."

The armored car groaned forward. Jean tried to get comfortable, but her wrists were lashed behind her back with thin strips of plastic. Somewhere in the distance Mike Wallace was arguing with an officer who had ordered the camera crew's equipment confiscated. The caravan began to roll. With the exception of her wedding day, Jean could not remember feeling more happy.

Jean Gump receives hundreds of letters every month from all over the world, most of them praising her for the actions she and other Plowshare activists have taken to resist and, they hope, end the arms race. Articles about her have appeared in important newspapers and national magazines, and a film is being made about Jean and her family. Nevertheless, she insists, people who do Plowshare actions are not all that special. Just look at our own nation's history, Jean suggests. We would still be living under British tyranny if no one had protested the Tea Act of 1773, if Samuel Adams's followers hadn't disguised themselves as Indians and dumped $75,000 worth of tea into the Boston Harbor. Didn't some members of the Virginia assembly cry "Treason" when Patrick Henry told them that "Caesar had his Brutus; Charles I his Cromwell; and George III may profit by their example"? The Declaration of Independence was an incendiary, revolutionary document, not a modest proposal or call to reform. Thomas Paine, Patrick Henry, and Benjamin Franklin were not talking about reform, weren't interested in letter-writing campaigns or tea-party diplomacy. They were revolutionaries, radicals, fighting one of the most powerful nations on earth at the time. We enshrine them in our history books, but have always imprisoned people who truly try to practice their ideals, citizens who want to really live, not just read about, the Founding Fathers' ideas and ideals.

People, says Jean, have been resisting tyranny and protesting crimes of government for centuries. This is particularly true now, when there is no moral discussion in this country or elsewhere on war, poverty, homelessness, and the environment. Just great praise for pro-democracy movements abroad, and the same old corruption and demagoguery at home.

"But, in truth, you see, Plowshare activists are far more dangerous to the U.S. government than any rapist or mass-murderer or terrorist. Because we are promoting an idea that is so very contrary to our national policy. We're promoting *nonviolence*. A dangerous concept articulated two thousand years ago by the man to whom millions of Americans pay homage every Sunday, including men and women who spend the rest of the week designing or building weapons of mass destruction. To a nation that believes [that] everything, every problem, every dispute can be resolved through violence, the Plowshares activists are very, very dangerous. We're a violent nation. We believe, absolutely, in violence. Put people in prison. Put people to death. Send our youth to war. Torture the poor so they'll want to be rich. Carry handguns. Blow people away. That's our creed, our motto, our belief system.

"The government argues we need more prisons. You know, the more prisons, the less crime. But the truth is, the more prisons, the more crime. Take the death penalty, for example. Whenever the state is willing to take a human life, the crime rate soars. Whether the state's willing to gas, electrocute, strangle, or shoot murderers, the killings proliferate. Because violence never stops violence. It only begets more violence. Always.

"We're a vindictive society. We want to get even when somebody does us harm. But I can tell you from being in prison that all anyone learns in a place like this is more criminal skills than they ever knew before. I mean," she laughs, "I know so many things now that I never knew before I came here. Never. Like how to get dope and drugs. And I'm not even in the market for them, but anybody who is in that market will develop the right contacts in prison. And ply their trade once they get out."

By prison standards, Jean's job in Alderson's greenhouse is almost a sinecure, definitely a reprieve from the robotized monotony most inmates endure. Still, as she bends over the rows of potted plants, tending an African violet with loving care, repotting a geranium, or watering a few struggling marigolds, Gump often hears gunfire just a short distance away.

"I mean," she says, waving to her left, "I'm over in the greenhouse putting my flowers together, a marvelous job really, and *bang! bang! bang!* Everybody who works for this institution has to practice shooting. It's part of their job descriptions, and they must spend some time on the shooting range. Because, in the event of a national emergency, the inmates have to be shot. Now, that puts one off balance a little. Listening to those guns, and knowing that, without doubt, they might some day be used on you. Even dentists, doctors, and nurses practice shooting, but they will tell you it's just part of the routine. There probably won't be a national emergency, so they really won't have to shoot us.

"But do you see what that would do to your mindset? Let's say that you are a doctor or a nurse, maybe a teacher, and you come in here, and you're teaching. Then they say, 'Well, part of your job is to practice firing at human-like targets, so that in the event of an emergency you can kill your students, or patients.' The really funny part is that the shooting won't occur 'unilaterally.' All '2-levels,' for example, will only get shot in the knees. Oh yes, the authorities have different categories. And I just keep thinking that I should put a sign on my chest saying: HEY, I'M JUST AN ORDINARY 1-LEVEL. I DON'T NEED TO BE KILLED IN THE EVENT OF A NATIONAL EMERGENCY."

Why hasn't she just packed up a few things and headed for some island in the North Sea, someplace where she might sit by the turf fire, listening to the roar of wind and sea, a good book on her lap, cup of tea or glass of white wine in hand. Someplace where the land is not seeded with thousands of Hiroshimas?

"Because," she answers without hesitation, "I like America. It's my country. And I like the people, not the government. Where do you think we'd be if Ben Franklin had decided to stay in France when he visited there, Martin Luther King, Jr., had become an expatriate, Malcolm X had immigrated to Africa, the suffragettes had sailed away to some more peaceful setting, the abolitionists had retired to Canada? The list goes on and on. Plowshare activists are just the heirs to a long, noble line of resisters, people who've been willing to stand up to government corruption, racism, the oppression of women, to go to jail and even give their lives for what they believe in. And besides, why give the country away to a handful of greedy people who already think they own it? The super-wealthy, not the people, really do control the political process, and *we're all in prison.* Some of us just a little more obviously than others. I mean, I'm more in prison than you because there's a fence out there, and I can't just walk out the gate today. But you're also in prison because you're working and paying for something you really don't believe in. It's called taxation without representation. And one time we had a Boston Tea Party on that issue, as I recall. And then a revolution.

"See, the psychology of the government is that it must, through various types of intimidation, keep people living in terror of what can be done to them if they don't conform, pay their taxes, keep a low profile, remain an anonymous source at all times. That's why we Plowshare activists are in prison. It has nothing, absolutely nothing, to do with the amount of damage we do, which is always insignificant. Nothing to do with money. I mean, it will cost the American taxpayers $300,000 to keep me in prison, for a mere $428.48 fine. Does that make sense? We're political prisoners. Prisoners of conscience. Kin to the Soviet refuseniks, only the Soviet Union has made some progress with their political dissidents. We haven't. We Plowshare activists are in prison for what we say about the United States, about violence, the arms race, poverty, how our government officials squander our natural resources, talent, and money, and how this nation is anything but a democracy. An aristocracy, perhaps. An oligarchy, corporate Fascism, call it what you will. But not democracy. The government just has to keep us quiet.

Shut us away. Buried alive. And doesn't all the time, money, and energy they spend doing that say something? Doesn't that somehow prove our point?"

Twelve hundred miles away, Joe Gump is completing a forty-month sentence at the federal penitentiary for men in Sandstone, Minnesota. An assistant warden brings us coffee in a silver thermos, and three styrofoam cups. On one wall is a plaque

U.S. Parole Commission
Department of Justice
*Qui Pro Domina Justitia Sequitur*

and an eagle, arrows in one claw, olive branch in the other. In the statement he left at the missile site where he and Jerry Ebner had gone to beat swords into plowshares, Joe had declared: "We cannot believe a government which, while negotiating reductions in European-based nuclear warheads, simultaneously seeks ways of converting the warheads for deployment to other locations. This is neither disarmament nor arms reduction.

"We resist a government which budgets 65 billion dollars for deployment of a thousand strategic warheads on mobile rail and truck launchers based on Whitman and other air force bases while telling its citizens that it genuinely wants arms reductions.

"We say 'No' to a government which stimulates the economy by authorizing 90 million dollars to prepare runways at Whitman Air Force Base for the Stealth bomber while ignoring the farmers whose family lands are taken from them because of budget constraints."

The court heard Joe's story—a chemical engineer, devout

Catholic, law-abiding citizen, almost a true believer. During visits to Germany he had asked relatives about the Holocaust trains: Who drove them? Who fired their engines, coupled their cars, kept them in running order? Who manufactured the cyanide gas, strung the barbed wire, built the crematoria? And what about the odor that must have stung the nostrils of even the most ostrich-headed worshiper on Sunday mornings? Did no one see the fires leaping from those tall chimneys? Who typed the lists of those to be deported? Who rounded up the children? Who herded them into eternity? Who? His hosts would sigh. Yes, even good people can get caught up in evil. Even good people sometimes look the other way. Joe told the court about visiting one of the 150 missile sites that ring Kansas City, Missouri. How the farmers in that region merely shrug, preferring, they say, to be killed outright in a nuclear war. About how, as he listened to testimony at his wife's Plowshare trial, the world had begun to shift in and out of focus. How he had decided to stop driving the trains, firing the engines, ignoring the pleas of the human cargo in those boxcars. His nostrils burned. He could no longer look the other way. He took a hammer, pounding, pouring blood. . . .

"No," says Joe Gump. "Obviously I don't think I'm crazy. And I don't spend a lot of time judging people. That's not what I'm in here for. But it seems to me that anyone who stands by and doesn't do anything at all—they've got to have their own sanity questioned. Is a person acting rationally if he or she denies the peril they are facing? Is it sane to pretend the arms race is over? Does it make sense to believe people, like Mr. Bush, who have always made their living telling lies?

"Of course I realize that not all Christians would agree

with what Plowshare activists do, or with what Jean and I have done. Some even seem to be actively involved in bringing war about, working in plants that assemble the three to five nuclear warheads we produce in this country each day. But I just don't understand how they can find this kind of work compatible with the teachings of Christ, who admonished Peter to replace the ear of the soldier, to put down the sword, love God and, most important, love our enemies. How could the use of nuclear weapons possibly be an act that God would approve of? How could killing hundreds of millions of people be compatible with the teachings of Christ? And how could destroying the planet, whether through actual use of, or simply building nuclear weapons—because building them is destroying the planet—have anything to do with Christianity? It can't. It won't. It never has, never will."

Visiting hours are over and Sandstone's inmates must be counted, fed, and sent to bed. A woman walks through the metal detector, weeping and clutching her purse. The parking lot is baking, heat rising in waves that make it difficult to walk. The woman turns, as though hoping to see her husband following. He does not appear.

# *Notes*

1. Thomas Merton, *Raids On The Unspeakable* (New York: New Directions, 1964), 46–7.

2. Ibid.

3. Pope John XXIII, *Pacem in Terris,* quoted in *Blessed are the Peacemakers,* (New York: Popular Library, 1971), 85–6.

4. United States Catholic Conference of Bishops, "Pastoral Letter On Nuclear War," quoted in Laurence Behrens and Leonard J. Rosen, eds., *Writing and Reading Across the Curriculum,* Second Edition (Boston: Little Brown, 1985), 514.

5. Ibid., 521.

# Four

## *Dungeons and Dragons: Plowshare Activists and the U.S. Judicial System*

In a desperate situation of utter powerlessness, a minority with deep moral and religious convictions has the duty to speak up, and even more, to resist in whatever form necessary.

DOROTHEE SOLLE

Cold. Slivers of glass grinding against her instep, working the length of her calves, along her back, as though looking for some place to drive in deep, some fatal port of entry. She caught her breath, exhaling softly, the mist floating off into darkness. At their meetings they had joked about it: "So what if the fence really does part for us? You know, stands aside like the Red Sea and lets us in." And here it was—not a particularly large hole but sufficient to crawl through, almost an invitation to enter this great sprawling base.

So quiet. The machines squatting in rows, like fairytale beasts dozing after a meal of succulent young children. Nodding. Indifferent to the four intruders who would soon

83

hammer their way inside, smashing instrument panels, spraypainting slogans, and pouring their own blood over interiors.

Lin Romano and Father Dexter Lanctot slipped through the breach and waited for Father Thomas McGann and former army lieutenant Greg Boertje, but Father McGann had never climbed a fence, and got caught in the barbed wire, a perfect target for an alert guard. There would be a sharp crack, something tearing loose, strips of cloth ripping, magnified and reverberating off the night. *Thump*, then the snow turning pink. Screams, flashing lights, curses, and scalpels and IVs. A blood-stained sheet pulled slowly over the astonished, still-open eyes. The intruders were dressed in black, but it had snowed during the night, and, bobbing across the white expanse of Willow Grove Naval Air Station, they looked like giant tar-coated rabbits.

There was no shot. Thomas wiggled loose from the wire, and they moved toward the beasts, snow crunching underfoot like cellophane. Lin and Dexter tried the doors on an aircraft that carries nuclear depth charges and is used to track Soviet submarines, but they were locked. Still no guards, no shouts or sirens. They poured blood over the Navy insignia, cut through the hydraulic lines and waited. No one. Dexter hoisted himself upon the metal stairs of the P-3 Orion, hammered off the small Master padlock that clasped the doors, then stepped inside. Lin joined him and they poured more blood, pounded on the control panel, and flipped open the Bible Lin was carrying. The passage, chosen at random, read:

The wicked shall draw their swords, but they shall pierce their own hearts.

Overwhelmed by yet another coincidence, Lin and Dexter hugged, then descended to the tarmac and waited to be arrested.

Cold. Heavy duty now, planting itself solidly in her boots, her arms and feet aching, her nose so cold it would snap off if lightly touched. They prayed, walked in circles, hung their banner—SEEK THE DISARMED CHRIST—from the doorway of the damaged aircraft, awaited the soft *pop* of a flare, the sky filling with giant white squid whose tentacles would flail briefly before tumbling languidly toward the snow-crusted earth. No sound at all, only the wind nosing softly around the aircraft, stars snapping off and on, the moon a thin shard of yellow glass hanging, it appeared, directly over Philadelphia. They had entered quite close to the control tower, walking unchallenged to the planes, walking and banging, banging and walking, and now they stood on the runway, slightly dazed with the ease of it all.

Lin reentered the plane to retrieve a baby bottle that had contained her own blood, heard Dexter talking to someone outside the plane, and marveled at the tricks cold and darkness played on one's senses. The security guard asked, "Who are you?" And Dexter replied, "Well, we're nonviolent protesters, and we're here to disarm these aircraft." The guard turned away, holding her radio to her ear, shaking it a couple of times before announcing, "There're a couple of nuts out here, over."

"Oh, no," Dexter corrected. "We're not nuts."

The security guard blinked, nodded, spoke into the radio. "Oh, well, I've got a couple of nonviolent protesters out here."

Security arrived, friendly young Americans coming to

capture other friendly Americans. No handcuffs or searches, no threats or recriminations. In the office where Lin and Dexter were held, guards read the protesters' leaflets, smoked, and sipped coffee. It was very warm and the guards were relaxed, curious, almost pleased at this break in their nightly routine. Ten minutes passed, fifteen, then half an hour before someone finally asked:

"Did you come alone?"

"Well, no," Romano replied. "As a matter of fact we did not."

Under a bright spotlight, holding their banner as steady as their shivering bodies could manage, Greg Boertje and Father McGann were finally arrested, grateful that someone had come to take them out of the cold.

A member of Naval security finally did arrive and he was furious, ordering that the demonstrators be handcuffed. They were held in a room for the next nine hours. A succession of young officers guarded Lin and friends, listening with great interest as the protesters explained why they had come to Willow Grove Naval Station, what they hoped to accomplish, and why they were willing to go to jail for this "symbolic" action.

"Holy Toledo," said one of the young guards, pointing to Dexter. "We could have shot you. Don't you know? We have orders to shoot to kill if we see anyone doing that kind of stuff. And we wouldn't have known who you were, and, heavens, *you're a Catholic priest!*"

"Oh, my God," said another guard. "My grandmother's gonna kill me when she hears I arrested a priest."

Thomas and Greg were kept in separate offices, questioned, and asked to give statements. Later, they would tell Lin and Dexter that, from their own position half a mile across the base they had been able to hear loud hammering, and couldn't understand why security hadn't come running immediately. As had been and would be the case in all Plowshare actions, the demonstrators found it easy to enter a "secure facility" and, most remarkably, to complete their plans without anyone being hurt. In one of the group's role-playing sessions before their action, Dexter had been shot, forcing Lin and the others to acknowledge that one of the consequences of beating swords into plowshares could be serious injury or death. During more than a decade of Plow-share actions at Strategic Air Command bases, missile sites, and submarine bases, no one has ever been injured or killed.

The FBI arrived, but Lin and the other members of the Epiphany Plowshares refused to speak to them. Over and over, Lin, Greg, and the two priests asked to call their attor-ney, concerned that friends might think something had gone wrong, possibly that they'd been injured or even killed. Their requests were denied. Morning crawled toward afternoon, the handcuffs remained on and the protesters were given no food. Pain crept from wrist to elbow, elbow to mid-arm to shoulder, spreading like the poison from an abscessed tooth, then localizing in the shoulder sockets. The clock stood still. It was as if a team of Clydesdales had been attached to each arm and whacked on their enormous haunches. But in spite of the pain, isolation, and hunger, the four were happy. They had breached the gates of this "killing ground," broken through their own fears, and acted out the Biblical impera-tive to beat swords into plowshares.

On the way to Philadelphia, the FBI agents were cordial, even friendly, asking Romano to tell them who gave her a ride to Willow Grove Naval Air Station, who helped the pro-testers plan their action, who offered them advice. The car droned softly through Warminister, Abington, Glenside. Lin looked out at the rows of trim little houses, their lawns dusted with snow and lights glowing warmly in their windows. Could the families in these snug suburban homes ever believe what their own government was planning? A Holocaust that would kill not six million but hundreds of millions of people *in the very first half hour.* What if, having been invited into one of these living rooms, she were to try telling the occupants that the gas chambers were already in place, the ovens started up, and all of us just hoping against hope?

The driver glanced in the rear-view mirror, and noticed that Lin was smiling. How much she would like to hire a skywriter to sweep her thoughts across the rooftops of Philadelphia, from the scented boutiques of Society Hill to the crack houses of North Philly, from the brothels of Center City to the antebellum mansions of Bryn Mawr SWORDS INTO PLOWSHARES, the little Piper Cub would unfold over Reading Terminal. CHOOSE LIFE, over the Franklin Institute. FEED THE POOR, NOT THE PENTAGON, the plane would proclaim, crisscrossing the Italian Market, out over the Naval Yard, up and down the Schuylkill River until the sky became a patchwork quilt of hope.

Lin Romano was twenty years old, a student in good standing at the University of Maryland, when she decided to leave college. She began working full time in a medical hospitality house sponsored by the Community For Creative Nonviolence in Washington, D.C. One night, a seventy-eight-year-old woman who had been beaten and raped showed up. Another, a retarded man whose frostbitten leg had recently been amputated appeared asking for help. Just a stone's throw from the White House, elderly people refused admission to hospitals were freezing to death, curled up on the sidewalk like emaciated fetuses. Most distressing to Lin were the homeless children, with their huge frightened eyes, thin coats, and hopeless shrugs. At first slowly, and then with astonishing speed, the number of hungry, destitute, and homeless had begun to grow, but few people seemed to notice and fewer still appeared to care. One day Lin came across some interesting figures: The cost of one Trident nuclear submarine, $1.7 billion, was enough to restore full funding for food stamps. $11 billion would compensate for cuts in subsidized housing or fund the cruise missile program. $1.3 billion would make up for the Reagan administration's cuts in mass transit subsidies or build six B-1 bombers. $40 billion would restore cuts in health, education, and training programs, or pay for the development of a first-strike missile system.[1]

The problem was not whether the government had the money to feed the hungry or house the homeless, but how the President and Congress chose to spend our taxes. Death, it appeared, always prevailed over life, war over peace, violence over nonviolence. Lin walked rapidly, swinging her arms, allowing her anger to rise and fall. A limousine, long, black, and sleek, raced by. Sirens wailed. A jet swooped over the Potomac. Down the block, two teenage drug dealers stood sentry in front of a boarded-up house; a young woman in a mini-dress and six-inch heels nodded into the ozone; and an old man wrapped in cardboard and a grease-stained blanket lay sleeping, or dead, in a burned-out doorway.

With each new budget cut, each assault on the nation's poor, the streets were getting meaner, drugs and violence spreading, jails, psychiatric units, and morgues overflowing.

Along with others from the Community for Creative Non-violence, Lin sought to open a dialogue with the White House, but was ignored. Sometimes CCNV activists knelt on the President's lawn, praying and waiting to be arrested. Mitch Snyder, community organizer and spokesperson for the homeless, fasted for fifty days, awakening from a coma to discover that President Reagan had promised five million dollars to help renovate a shelter for the homeless. Snyder recovered and, after some delays, the money arrived.

When it was particularly cold or snowed, Lin and others attended services at St. Matthew's Cathedral and the Episcopal National Cathedral, where they would announce that people were dying on the streets of the nation's capital, freezing to death quite literally on the steps of the city's churches. "Now, these people have no place to go tonight," Lin would announce, pointing to the homeless men and women standing beside her. "So we suggest that at the end of this service you allow them to sleep here, in your church. Surely our Lord, Jesus Christ, would welcome them. Surely *He* would not put them out. Just open your hearts and your doors, that's all we're asking. Give them shelter." The parishioners refused. Priests, bishops, ministers refused. The White House refused. Congress refused.

One week, after several homeless people were found frozen to death on the streets, Lin and a homeless man walked to the pulpit during petitions for prayers, expropriating the microphone and announcing that at that very moment people were dying, or would soon die, because St. Matthew's refused to open its doors to the poor. Then, as the astonished worshipers looked on, Lin and her companion poured blood over the linen-draped altar. Ushers rushed forward, someone cried for help, Lin and her companion were grabbed, pushed, pulled, and squeezed in a bear hug until the police arrived to charge them with disrupting a religious service. For the homeless, jail was at least a way to keep from freezing to death.

Lin continued to work with the homeless, but in spite of the joy she derived from helping others, she felt uneasy at times, even troubled. Was it really enough, she asked herself, to be working with victims of military spending? Shouldn't she go straight to the cause, indeed resist the very *root* of the evil? She was familiar with Plowshare actions, respected the people who did such things, and wondered if this might be one very direct and positive way to challenge Reagan's obsessive militarism.

Yet she also knew that scattered across the nation were people who had been sentenced to five, ten, even eighteen years in prison for pouring blood over or slightly damaging nuclear weapons components (no one had ever actually damaged a nuclear weapon). The years with CCNV had passed quickly and she was almost thirty, thinking a lot about having children, wanting a family of her own. Jail was not the issue. She had already been locked up many times for her advocacy of the poor, but ten years, 3,650 days, was something altogether different. Would she be able to have children when she was forty? After a decade in a federal penitentiary, would she be physically and spiritually intact enough to have a family?

Lin thought and prayed. Certainly she had all the right excuses for not engaging in a Plowshare action: *She could accomplish more outside of prison. She deserved to have children. She would not allow the legal system to control her life. The poor and homeless really needed her.* But millions of children were starving to death while she sat pondering her own fate, dying because the world's governments chose to squander trillions of dollars each year on military hardware. So many children going to bed at night without knowing if the world would still be here in the morning, children who deserved to be dreaming of sugarplums instead of mushroom clouds. Were they not her responsibility? Should she not do something immediate, something consistent with her concerns and her religious faith, to say no to this slaughter of the innocents?

Before their first trial for the Willow Grove action, the Epiphany Four met to discuss nonviolence, their religious beliefs, and international law. Sometimes they tried to imagine what might actually transpire in the courtroom. Would the judge, as most had done in previous Plowshare trials, simply refuse to allow them to call expert witnesses who could verify the threat nuclear weapons pose to world peace and the survival of the world? Witnesses, for example, like former Lockheed weapons designer Robert Aldridge, who describes the Trident nuclear submarine as the "most destructive weapon in history," and calls the captain of a Trident "the third most powerful man in the world," a man who controls "more destructive force than all the other nations combined."[2] Or Yale psychiatrist and author Robert Jay Lifton, who would tell the judge and jury that "Survivors of a nuclear blast wouldn't just envy the dead. They would actually behave as if dead. Survivors would not really feel alive. In other words, there is no psychological capacity to prepare for, or survive, nuclear weapons."[3] And George Wald, Nobel Prize–winner in biology, who would say that, "Life has never been as threatened in the entire history of our planet. . . . The present stockpiles of the U.S. and the

Soviet Union are about the equivalent of sixteen billion tons of TNT. There are four billion people on earth, so that means about four tons of TNT for every man, woman, and child on the earth. So there's a good chance that by now we've already stockpiled all the nuclear hardware necessary to wipe out the human race, and much of the rest of life on this planet, the very first 'do it yourself' extinction."[4]

If permitted to do so, the Epiphany protesters would describe how U.S.-trained soldiers in El Salvador routinely beat, torture, rape, and execute their fellow countrymen and women. If the judge did not clear the courtroom, as judges in other Plowshare trials had done, the Epiphany Four might talk about the body dumps where vultures peck out the eyes of the "disappeared," and how the mutilated and tortured corpses turn up in vacant lots, ravines, public restrooms, and even bus stations. And Puerta del Diablo, where the death squads torture and gang-rape their victims before killing them and tossing their bodies over the precipice. Later, when relatives or friends of the victims climb down the cliff looking for remains, helicopters often hover overhead. Made-in-America aircraft, Romano would tell the court, threatening the *mothers* of the disappeared; trained-in-America pilots harassing mothers who, if they were not careful, might soon join their sons and daughters at the bottom of Puerta del Diablo.

The first Epiphany Plowshare trial began on March 16, 1987, ending just a week later when the jurors returned deadlocked after deliberating for several days. Judge Raymond J. Broderick allowed the defendants to talk, albeit briefly, about their motives for going to Willow Grove, their religious faith, and their belief that the world is locked into a life-and-death struggle. The jury listened closely, sorting and scrutinizing, but later could not break its deadlock.

After the first trial, government prosecutors approached the defendants with a proposition, asking that Lin and friends plead guilty to one felony. If they agreed to do so, the prosecution would drop the other misdemeanor and felony charges. After the second trial also resulted in a hung jury, the prosecution suggested the defendants plead guilty to a misdemeanor trespass in exchange for the government's dropping both felony charges. Greg and Lin refused to agree to plead guilty because, they explained, they were not. But Tom and Dexter had already suffered some rather serious consequences for their part in the action. While still in jail awaiting trial, Tom had heard that the archbishop wanted to see him. Accepting bail, he went straight to the chancery, where he was informed that he'd been suspended from his priestly duties. Two weeks later, Dexter also left jail, only to discover that he'd been evicted from his rectory, thrown out of his parish, and suspended from the archdiocese. Although neither had been convicted of a crime, the church convicted them, telling them their actions were "a scandal to the people in the archdiocese and to God."

Tom and Dexter decided to accept the government's offer and to plead guilty, but in very couched terms. Dexter was very careful to say, "Well, yes, by *your* laws I can see how *you* might construe that I am guilty, but in fact the way we see it is that we're not guilty." The judge accepted that as a guilty plea, and sentenced him to 100 days in jail. Tom was also sentenced to 100 days in prison.

As the third trial opened, with Lin Romano and Greg Boertje as defendants and Judge Broderick again presiding, tensions were building in the courtroom. Essential to any case Plowshare activists might make, and an argument consistently disallowed by U.S. judges, is the "necessity defense," a good example of which would be someone breaking into a burning building to save a child. Would that individual, Plowshare defendants would ask, be tried for burglary and/or breaking and entering? If the world is on fire, shouldn't someone be trying to put it out, even if this means violating the law? If the planet is about to be destroyed, shouldn't someone be trying to save it, even if their actions result in damaging property?

What if, for example, one had tried to cut the fence at Auschwitz? Or, seeing lines of weeping women and children, one had damaged the cyanide containers that were being used to kill them? And what if German resisters, discovering lists of Jews about to be deported to Buchenwald or Bergen-Belsen, had burned the paper on which these names were written? In Adolph Hitler's Third Reich, such acts were capital crimes, but would history consider the perpetrators criminals or heroes? Would history say they should have obeyed the law? Interesting and provocative questions, judges in Plowshare trials concede, but to use the necessity defense a defendant must demonstrate that certain things have been established:

- That the criminal conduct of which the defendants stand accused was taken to prevent a greater harm to themselves or others, which was imminent
- That there was no effective legal alternative method or course of action available to them that could be taken to avert this so-called harm, and

- That there was a direct causal relationship between the criminal conduct taken and the avoidance of the alleged harm

It is not necessary that the steps be completely effective in order to use this defense; in other words, it wouldn't be necessary that they destroyed all nuclear weapons, but that they had an effect upon them.[5]

Judge Broderick refused to allow the necessity defense and, after the first two trials ended in hung juries, accepted the government's *motion in limine* to exclude all testimony he considered unrelated to the charges of conspiring to damage U.S. property, entering a military institution for an unlawful purpose, and damaging four aircraft.

To assure that testimony before the jury was limited to these specific charges, and to avoid any discussion of the defendants' motives for going to Willow Grove Naval Air Station, Judge Broderick prepared a list of things that could not be mentioned or discussed in front of the jury without his permission. Any attempt to talk about these things, he informed the defendants, would result in a contempt citation and perhaps time in jail. The list was as follows:

1. U.S. nuclear arms policy
2. The amount of funds allocated in the U.S. budget for nuclear arms, instruments of war, defense, social services and/or welfare
3. U.S. foreign policy in Central America, the Middle East or elsewhere
4. The conduct of President Reagan, Vice President Bush, President Reagan's cabinet or former cabinet members,

present or former members of the National Security
Council, the Joint Chiefs of Staff, Congress, or the CIA

5. Principles of international law, including but not limited
   to:
   a. Nuremberg principles and/or any provision of the
      Nuremberg Charter
   b. Any provision of the United Nations Charter
   c. Any provision of the Geneva Convention; and
   d. Any rulings of the International Court at The Hague

6. Any person or group's understanding of the word of
   God; and

7. Any religious, moral or ethical convictions relating to
   nuclear weapons, nuclear war, foreign policy, war in
   general, disarmament and/or fear of a nuclear holocaust[6]

In addition to disallowing the necessity defense and accepting the government's *motion in limine,* Judge Broderick
told Lin and Greg that they would not be permitted to call
expert witnesses. Unlike Federal Judge Howard G. Munson
who allowed expert witnesses to testify in the Griffiss Plowshare trial, then instructed the jury to disregard everything
they'd heard, Broderick made it clear that he would not have
expert witnesses in his courtroom. Obviously weary and
frustrated after the first two trials had ended inconclusively,
Judge Broderick also said that the jury would not be allowed
to hear character witnesses or "specific instances of character." Lin Romano's commitment to the homeless or whether
or not Greg and Lin were acting out of a deep sense of commitment to, and belief in, the Gospels was irrelevant. In this
trial, testimony would be limited to, ". . . the standard ques-

tions which are asked in all criminal trials . . . you know, how long you have known him or do you know the defendants.

"How long you have known them and do you have an opinion as to the defendant's character for being a law-abiding citizen or something else that is relevant to the particular trial and then also, whether you know other people that know him and what is their reputation for, in this instance, being law-abiding citizens."

Concluding his remarks, Judge Broderick warned the defendants, "There is no point in winning the battle with the jury and losing it by being found in contempt. I'm not doing this," he added, "to threaten you."

"I think we might disagree with that," Greg Boertje replied. Boertje would be found in contempt of court several times before the government argued for, and was granted, a mistrial.[7]

When they are tried for entering military installations and pouring their own blood over or pounding on missiles and airplanes, Plowshare activists argue that our government is about to violate, or is already violating, certain international treaties which limit the scope of, or prohibit, warfare. For example, beginning with the Hague conventions in 1899 and 1907, the U.S. and some European nations attempted to work out agreements on the rules of warfare, i.e. prohibitions against the indiscriminate slaughter of innocent civilians. In August 1928, France and forty-two other nations went even further, signing the Pact of Paris, or Kellogg-Briand Pact, that "condemns recourse to war for the solution of international controversies," and renounces war as an instrument of the policy of nations "in their relations with one another."[8] Article 2 of the pact states, "The High Contracting Parties agree that the settlement or solution of all disputes or conflicts, of whatever nature or whatever origin they may be, which may arise among them, shall never be sought except by pacific means."[9] So important was this concept of limiting force to self-defense, that the United Nations adopted it as the "cornerstone of modern international law governing the use of force . . ."[10]

In arguing their case before federal judges, Plowshare defendants consistently point to these treaties as a legitimate framework for citizen participation in resisting or attempting to prevent crimes of state. To substantiate their argument that citizens have not only the right but the duty to break the law if they are convinced such actions are in the best interests of peace, they ask judges and juries to consider the International Tribunal's judgment at Nuremberg, which states:

> Individuals have international duties which transcend the national obligations of obedience imposed by the individual state. He who violates the laws of war cannot obtain immunity while acting in pursuance of the authority of the state if the state in authorizing action moves outside its competence under international law.[11]

The importance of the Nuremberg and Tokyo trials at the end of World War II, says Richard Falk, Milbank Professor of International Law at Princeton University, is that they were "landmark developments that planted seeds of new understanding on the part of citizens as to their political obligations. The Nuremberg concept was extended down the ladder of responsibility from the level of primary leaders, and applied to doctors, judges, and business executives who were associated with implementing one or another facet of officially sanctioned Nazi (and Japanese imperial) policies. The logic of Nuremberg is even wider, suggesting that anyone with knowledge of crimes of state has a responsibility to act to prevent their continuation, and that no superior order or sense of nationalistic identity should inhibit this primary duty."[12]

U.S. lawyers and judges helped articulate these guidelines for citizen conduct; however, writes Dr. Falk, our government's response to Plowshare actions has been:

> one of procedural preemption, namely, that the citizen has no standing to invoke international law in relation to foreign policy, and beyond this, that the court has neither the competence nor the constitutional mandate to pass legal judgement. The disallowance of the international law argument is often reinforced in a highly contrived way by disallowing expert testimony, especially with a jury present (most judges are quite adept at listening without hearing when the occasion warrants), and by delivering jury instructions that seek to limit the assessing role of the uncontested facts of the symbolic violation of domestic law, giving the jury no space within which to return an acquittal based on the contested facts of violation of international law.[13]

As the third trial progressed, Judge Broderick and Greg Boertje clashed repeatedly over procedural rules and just what could and could not be said in front of the jury. In his opening statements, Boertje referred to the "crimes that the government is committing at Willow Grove Naval Air Station," and the prosecuting attorney promptly objected.

Judge Broderick sustained the objection, calling Boertje to the bench and threatening him with contempt if he continued to violate the *motion in limine* restricting testimony. Boertje began again by telling the jury, "We went there and we conspired to do what the law prohibits, and we say, we went there and conspired to do *what the law requires.* . . . People must stand up and do something to stop bloodshed and in the Bible, which everyone put their hands on . . ." *Objection!* Sustained.

At the sidebar, Boertje told the judge that his restrictions on testimony were tantamount to a "gag order," and "remind us of a situation in Germany under Hitler when the judges complied with the administration of the laws that Hitler made, and therefore were complicit and they were tried after the war for war crimes. And found guilty . . . We want to make it clear to you that you have the responsibility to abide by Nuremberg laws and not to be complicit with the war crimes of the Reagan administration."[14]

Judge Broderick warned Boertje that he was about to find him in contempt of court. The jury returned, and Boertje began:

"The evidence will show that in the Bible blood is not silent."

*Objection.* Sustained.

Judge Broderick told Boertje, "The Court's order is very clear that what is in the Bible is not a defense. We are not here to discuss or to consider the meaning of the Bible or what is the Law of God. We are here in connection with a violation of federal statutes and please continue along those lines."

The jury was again dismissed, and Greg found in contempt of court. When the jury returned, he began, "Before,

I was speaking about our understanding of the scriptures and had, what we had found in the scriptures, led us to this action and the government objected and we had a previous objection when I spoke about the crimes of the government that are going on at Willow Grove."

*Objection.* Sustained.

Jury dismissed, returned, informed by Judge Broderick that:

"Principles of international law are not relevant in this proceeding. . . . I also want to point out to you and this is by no way a complete list that such things as Nuremberg Principles, the United Nations Charter, Provisions of the Geneva Convention, Rulings of the International Court at The Hague, they are not admissible and they are not relevant in this trial.

"Another thing that the Court ruled was not relevant to the conduct of this trial was the defendants' or any person or any group's understanding of what is the word of God, what are the provisions in the Bible. What are the religious, the moral or ethical convictions relating to nuclear weapons, nuclear war, foreign policy, war in general, disarmament, fear of a holocaust, those things are not relevant."[15]

Boertje attempted to explain that he and Lin had studied international law with professors, U.S. judges, and judges from West Germany. Judge Broderick's ruling, he told the jury, was "invalid" because federal law is superseded by international law. Broderick responded by sustaining the prosecution's objection, dismissing the jury and finding Boertje in contempt of court once more. There were shouts of derision from spectators, and the judge ordered federal marshals to evict people from his courtroom. When the jury returned, Lin Romano commenced to cross-examine Lt. Commander William E. Dean, a security officer at Willow Grove Naval

Air Station. She asked if he had ever flown a P-3 Orion and, when he answered yes, she inquired:

"And are you aware that the P-3 Orion might be the first aircraft to deliver a nuclear bomb against a sub?"

The prosecution objected, and was sustained.

Lin asked Lt. Commander Dean if the U.S. Constitution is "part of" the Federal Magistrate System and he replied, "Not per se."

"In your opinion, the Constitution is not part of federal law?" Lin asked.

*Objection.* Sustained.

"Have you ever studied the laws about genocide?" Romano asked.

*OBJECTION!*

"I have not," the witness answered.

"You have not?" Romano asked. "Do you know it's unlawful to kill mass populations of people?"[16]

As the level of frustration rose on all sides, spectators shouted questions at the jury and openly questioned the judge. One group entered the courtroom wearing scarves and towels around their mouths to protest Judge Broderick's "gag order" and turned their backs on the judge when he began to speak, facing the jury and silently bowing their heads. Others sang, opened banners, or read from the indictment the Epiphany Four had left at Willow Grove charging President Reagan, Vice President Bush, and others with war crimes.

Judge Broderick ordered some of the spectators removed, and warned others they would be held in contempt of court, and the marshals waded in, twisting arms, shoving, pushing, dragging people into the halls. A woman stood up and shouted, "You know, Your Honor, my little girl goes to bed at night crying and asking if we're going to die in a nuclear war." Furious, the judge ordered the marshals to remove her from the courtroom and, as they were doing so, the child asked if they were going to jail. "No, honey," her mother replied. "Not right now."

After a short break, the defendants returned and were informed that the judge had decided to declare a mistrial. Lin argued against this decision, but was told that the jury was too prejudiced in the defendants' favor. After seeing a woman and her daughter dragged from the courtroom, the judge explained, it was highly unlikely that any jury would remain impartial. Thus ended the third trial of Epiphany Plowshare activists Lin Romano and Greg Boertje.

In the middle of their fourth trial, when it became apparent there would simply be no dialogue between the defendants and judge, no meaningful exchange or opportunity to explain why they risked their lives and their future to enter Willow Grove Naval Air Station, Lin and Greg simply walked out of the courtroom, leaving the bewildered jurors and angry judge behind. "We are not allowed to tell the truth," Lin told Judge Broderick. "We were just spectators, that's all. So if we're spectators, we're going to join the rest of the audience."

Lin and Greg walked toward the door, and the spectators began to sing. Broderick was screaming, "Get them out of the courtroom, get them all out of here." People held hands and began walking out when suddenly, realizing his mistake, the judge shouted, "*No, not the defendants!* Bring them back in here. Bring them back."

Reading the transcripts from, or actually attending, Plowshare trials, one is struck by how difficult it is for the participants—judges, lawyers, juries, and defendants—to find common ground on which to communicate. Everyone appears to be speaking the same language, yet with different dialects or exotic syntax. With extraordinary persistence, often risking contempt citations, Plowshare defendants attempt to argue that their actions were meant to be constructive, not destructive; loving, not hateful; inspiring, not accusatory; open and honest, not surreptitious or deceitful.

"Our intent," Elizabeth McAlister told Judge Howard G. Munson and the jury during the Griffiss Plowshare trial, "had no malice toward any individual . . . And our intention was not to damage property. Indeed, we ask ourselves, the court, our friends, what property? Nothing proper here to human life. Nothing fitting, suitable in institutions of megadeath. In truth, no property. Our purpose was that death be robbed for a change of the last word and to say that these instruments of death constitute improper work so that people might begin a new day in peace."[17]

Federal judges consistently reply that the defendants' motives have no bearing on their guilt, that juries must consider intent—that is, did the defendants actually *intend* to enter the base for unlawful reasons, *intend* to damage government property, and *intend* to break the law. To Plowshare activists, the courtroom is a forum where a national, and perhaps even international, debate over the fate of the world should be taking place. To most federal judges, whether the world is burning is irrelevant in determining the guilt of people charged with conspiracy to damage or actually damaging government property.

There have been some notable exceptions. In some cases, juries who've been allowed to hear expert witnesses have found the defendants not guilty as charged. In one case where defendants were allowed to argue that significant social and political changes—the abolition of slavery, workers' rights to organize, the right of blacks and women to vote, granting of civil rights to blacks—came about as a result of people's willingness to violate unjust laws, the trial judge listened attentively, then declared that the defendants:

> are of a mind that political persuasion, while it may be helpful, is not going to be effective. They cite experiences in the history of this country, and we're all familiar with them, and they're not only of recent history. They run through the course of our history, and sometimes the defendants of yesterday are the heroes of today . . .[18]

In a case in which twenty-two people were arrested for blocking the entrance to the Great Lakes Naval Training Center in Wake Forest, Illinois, the defendants were found not guilty by the jury after the presiding judge instructed members that:

- International law is binding on the United States and on the State of Illinois
- The use or threat of use of nuclear weapons is a war crime or an attempted war crime because such use would violate international law by causing unnecessary suffering, failure to distinguish between combatants and noncombatants, and poisoning targets by radiation[19]

The trial of the *United States* v. *Laforge and Katt* is also worth mentioning, not only because the defendants were allowed to use the necessity defense, but because of the statements Miles Lord, the presiding judge, made before sentencing the defendants to six months in jail, suspended on condition of six months' probation:

> It is the allegation of these young people that they committed the acts here complained of as a desperate plea to the American people and its government to stop the military madness which they sincerely believe will destroy us all, friend and enemy alike. . . . Can it be that those of us who build weapons to kill are engaged in a more sanctified endeavor than those who would counsel moderation and mediation as an alternative method of settling disputes?
>
> Why are we so fascinated by a power so great that we cannot comprehend its magnitude? What is so sacred about a bomb, so romantic about a missile? Why do we condemn and hang individual killers, while extolling the virtues of warmongers? What is the fatal fascination which attracts us to the thought of mass destruction of our brethren in another country? . . . I would here, in this instance, attempt in some way to force the government . . . to remove the halo—which it seems to hold over any device which can kill—and, instead, to place thereon a shroud, the shroud of death, destruction, mutilation, disease, and debilitation.[20]

After three frustrating attempts to send Greg and Lin to prison, the prosecution finally heard the jury foreman say "guilty" on all three counts—conspiracy, destruction of government property, and trespass, offenses for which the defendants might well be sentenced to fifteen years in prison. On November 17, 1987, Judge Raymond J. Broderick sentenced Lin Romano to two years and one hundred days in prison, and five years probation. "And Mr. Boertje?" Judge Broderick asked, glancing about the courtroom. "Not present," a federal marshal replied. A spectator standing nearby began to read from a single, double spaced sheet of paper:

"Our country is destroying itself," she read, "We worship the bloody god of military might. We are drunk on the blood that flows from Third World intervention and nuclear war preparation. . . . In Central America, we are responsible for the continued regional flow of innocent blood . . . going underground is a direct way to say no to the criminal courts which safeguard the blood crimes of our government."

Boertje's statement concluded with a kind of declaration of peace. Soon, said Boertje, he would "witness" again for peace by doing another nonviolent Plowshare action. As in the past, he would wait to be arrested, believing that "this course of action will fulfill the responsibility to resist death and to choose life."

"Well," Lin says. "I think one of the prosecutors summarized things appropriately when he said, 'If we don't convict you of something, it will look like a victory for the Plowshare movement.' I mean, they just wanted a conviction for anything, but if they thought prison would be a waste of time for me, they were totally wrong. I was able to do a lot of work for other inmates, and now the thought that they might put me away for five or ten years isn't an intimidating factor anymore."

And effectiveness? Lin sighs. How many times has she and other Plowshare activists been asked this question? As though there could be some kind of scorecard: *1* for the Plowshare team, *2* for the Pentagon, *3* for the defense (offense) industry. In a culture where everything—money, grades, job skills, intelligence, prestige, even love and sex—

is quantified, coded, given a numerical score, there must be some measurable way to determine the Plowshare Movement's success. Perhaps a card or two in Trivial Pursuit:

1. How many U.S. judges have been persuaded to leave the bench by Plowshare activists? *None.*
2. Why do some German judges consider the sentences given U.S. citizens for Plowshare actions to be barbaric? *Because, unlike their American counterparts, they understand the meaning of totalitarianism.*
3. Why have eight hundred West German judges and prosecutors formed an organization to oppose the arms race? *Because they believe in international law.*
4. Why do U.S. judges refuse to allow "jury nullification"?[21] *It would set a democratic precedent.*

"No," says Romano. "I don't try to measure the effectiveness of our action, because that just can't be done. But it was a very important turn in my life, one that I believe helped me face up to some fears, look them in the eye, and not back down from them. And there is a lot of education being done at those trials. For example, I received a letter from a member of the International Peace Walk who was invited to speak at the officers' wives' club at Willow Grove Naval Base. And the woman who invited this speaker said that she had gotten interested in the nuclear issue because of our action. So there were twenty-four, maybe thirty people there, including the officers and the base commander, all at this meeting. And the hostess said that, at first, she thought we were just a bunch of crazies, but then she began to think about it, wondering why we would go through these trials and willingly go to prison. And she concluded there must be some good reason why we were doing what we do, and later she even joined the Bucks County Alliance for Nuclear Disarmament.

Plowshare activists, says Romano, do not enjoy going to prison, are not martyrs, and do not sleep on beds of nails or wear hairshirts around the house. But, she says, "The INF Treaty hasn't done anything to stop the arms race. We're just proceeding full-tilt ahead, arming the heavens, arming the seas, putting new spy satellites into orbit, and always telling ourselves and everyone else on earth that we have a *right* to do this. That God has given us some kind of unique wisdom, some kind of ultimate mandate, to destroy creation. So how can I just go back to serving soup and bandaging wounds? Don't I need to continue in this vein? Unfortunately, there aren't very many people in this country still willing to do this kind of resistance. Not yet, anyway. So we have to continue either doing or supporting this type of action. And believe me, there's a great deal of openness to doing other things. I mean, we sit around all the time and say, 'Does anyone have a better idea?'" Lin pauses, laughs, looks about the room as though expecting an answer. "Because, if they do, we'd just love to hear it."

After nine months in prison, Lin Romano was released on appeal, but the government decided to try her once more. Her fifth trial resulted in a conviction for a misdemeanor, the maximum sentence for which would have been six months. "So," she laughs, "I had already done more time in prison than the sentencing guidelines allowed for. Like the court system itself, too ironic to be believed."

Greg Boertje surfaced on Easter Sunday, April 3, 1988, when he boarded the battleship *Iowa* at Norfolk Naval Station and, along with Philip Berrigan, Andrew Lawrence, and

Sister Margaret McKenna, commenced to hammer and pour blood on launchers for the Tomahawk cruise missile. Greg was sentenced to six months in jail for this action, served his time, and was then taken to a federal penitentiary to begin a thirty-three-month sentence for failing to appear before Judge Broderick on November 17, 1987. His original conviction for the Willow Grove action was overturned by the Pennsylvania Court of Appeals.

# Notes

1. *Feed the Cities, Not the Pentagon!* (a Flier) Womens League for Peace and Freedom, Philadelphia, Pa.

2. Sam Totten and Martha Wescoat Totten, eds. *Facing The Danger* (Trumansburg: The Crossing Press, 1984), 43.

3. *In The King of Prussia,* a film version of the Plowshare Eight Trial, directed by Emil De Antonio. Dr. Lifton was scheduled to give expert testimony at the trial, but was denied by the presiding judge, Samuel Salus III.

4. Ibid.

5. Arthur J. Laffin and Anne Montgomery, eds., *Swords into Plowshares* (New York: Harper & Row, 1987), 197.

6. *United States of America* v. *Gregory I. Boertje and Lin M. Romano,* Criminal No. 87-30, (*motion in limine* to exclude evidence of motive) July 10, 1987, 3.

7. *United States of America* v. *Gregory I. Boertje and Lin M. Romano,* Philadelphia, Pennsylvania. The Honorable Raymond J. Broderick, Sj. presiding, July 14, 1987, 7–9.

8. Telford Taylor, *Nuremberg and Vietnam: An American Tragedy* (New York: Bantam Books, 1970), 69–70.

9. Ibid.

10. Richard Falk, "The Extension of Law to Foreign Policy: The Next Constitutional Challenge," unpublished, 10.

11. Taylor, 84.

12. Falk, 10–11.

13. Ibid., 23.

14. *United States of America* v. *Boertje et al.,* July 14, 1987, 39.

15. Ibid., 48.

16. Ibid., 62–3.

17. Elizabeth McAlister, Testimony before Howard G. Munson, Griffiss Plowshare Action and Trial, Trial Sequences, Notes and Texts of Testimonies, Comment and News Coverage, 109.

18. *Swords Into Plowshares*, op. cit., 193.

19. Ibid., 195–6.

20. Ibid., 198.

21. Richard Falk, "The Spirit of Thoreau in the Age of Trident," *The Agni Review* 23, 1986, 39.

21. The underlying idea of trial by jury was to bring the conscience of the community to bear upon the application of the law. Thus, when the conscience of citizens is the essence of an alleged crime, there is a role for what is called "jury nullification," nullifying the law and acceding to claims of conscience. Our courts have generally tried to shut down this function of the jury, and to tie jurors' hands judges give legalistic instructions that disallow conscience to be taken into account, even in situations of symbolic criminality where the actions of those accused of lawlessness are motivated by citizens' fervor for a better society.

# Five

## Peace Warrior: The Transformation of a Vietnam Veteran

Hold out in defiance of all despotism.
GOETHE

I have become only remains that will be sent
to my family to identify, the sum of their
love, the total of their son.
WILLIAM CRAPSER

He stood on the edge of it, blinking, sweat pouring into his eyes, running past his ears, soaking his shirt until it stuck coldly to his back. "There it is, there it isn't. Is. Isn't. There . . . it . . . is . . ." The man beside him was pointing to something with his swagger stick, smiling, spreading his legs and putting his hands on his hips, hey, *Life,* put me on the cover. And everything was dead. Everything. He walked softly, as though not wishing to disturb the bloated bodies of water buffalo, scavenger birds plucking at their blackened entrails. To the right of the buffalo, a pile of rags, vague shapes, children siamesed together from the napalm's heat. "There it is," and, "No, there it can't be." He walked. The man beside him lighted a cigar, chewing and smiling, dipping to dust his spit-shined jump boots, wiping sweat from his brow with a blue silk scarf.

Heat was rising from the fly-covered corpses and burned hooches, charred pigs, water buffalo, children, babies. Inside, somewhere below his duodenum, deeper than his guts, anger bubbling first like fear or sickness then growing, tightening, swelling again, coming back to a small tight ball that threatened to burst out and . . . out where? Where could it go? A grenade launcher of anger, Gatling gun, M-16 on zip, he would fire it, let it explode, let it out, let it go, make it hit *them* . . . them? . . . who? . . . where? . . . how to find . . . *them?*

"This is bullshit." His tears mixed with the sweat. "Nuts, man. Dinky-dau, Dinky-fucking-dau."

He had always been a good boy. Born in Geneva, New York, July 4, 1941, moving to Chautauqua County when he was nine. His family was lower middle-class, very conservative, father in and out of different sales jobs. In school, he'd been an above-average student, good athlete, member of the Baptist Youth Fellowship and, like most of the boys in his town, a Boy Scout. The town was All American—250 residents, two feed mills, two general stores, farmers coming in on Saturdays to buy supplies, swap stories, predict the weather, and complain about or praise the growing season's yields. Boys rode bicycles through the streets, pitching papers at porches where ancient men and women sat in swings, cooling themselves with bamboo fans. In the schoolyard, boys played with and traded marbles, pure white and tabby-cat, tiger-striped and amethyst, preciously carried in cloth pouches tied in square knots to their belts. Girls jumped rope, threw jacks and hopscotched back and forth within chalked squares. Their hair, tied in pigtails and bright colored ribbons, flew like the manes of the circus ponies that came to town once a year. Time moved in slow motion, the Cold War little more than yesterday's byline, Vietnam a dot in some other, unimportant, galaxy.

In high school he kept a copy of J. Edgar Hoover's *Masters of Deceit,* along with the Bible, beside his bed. After supper, when the dishes were cleared away and the chairs placed in a half-circle, the family would gather to listen to Fulton Lewis, Jr., denounce Communists in government. And as Lewis called out the list of the nation's enemies, careful to enunciate each syllable in these foreign-sounding surnames, Brian's father would copy them down in his logbook, just in case—like Tom Joad or Preacher Casey in Steinbeck's "Communist novel"—one just happened to show up in this part of the country.

His father was in sympathy with the American Nazi party, admired its leader, George Lincoln Rockwell, and believed the Nazis were good and the Communists bad. In Geneva, New York, during World War II, his father had acted as an air-raid practice monitor, walking the streets during air-raid practices to make certain people turned their lights out until the "all clear" signal was given. Brian wanted to become an FBI agent when he grew up, dreaming, like many American boys his age, of tracking the nation's enemies down and locking them away in jail. After a lifetime of service, he would retire to a home draped with mementos of his fight against communism. His grandchildren would sit at his knees, listening to tales of shootouts, intrigue, agents and double agents, spies and counterspies. He would tell them that once upon a time the nation hovered at the brink, threatened with subversion from within and from without. But a man from Wisconsin by the name of Joseph McCarthy had seen the light when so many others appeared blinded by darkness. Without him, Brian Willson would tell his grandchildren, their own grandfather might also have been duped, and they might well be living in slavery.

In the Mekong Delta, Willson was occasionally requested to measure effectiveness, peruse the damage, take notes, make favorable reports. How would he draft it? Yes, very nice. Today we counted three scorched water buffalo, fourteen fried chickens, ten burned huts, eight parboiled ducks, two baked pigs, and numerous things that resembled charcoal briquets, things that a short time before had been breathing, laughing, alive, things that had wept when their children sickened or died, real people—giggling, holding hands, watching the moon roll out of the mists of a river or tumble down the slopes of a mountain, men and women sitting beside a stream that murmurs songs and poems about lotus flowers and steaming bowls of *pho*, the happiness at Tet, peace, reunification.

The village had been labeled a "free-fire zone," but the peasants refused to leave, disbelieving, perhaps, that anyone would do this to them—South Vietnamese pilots making three or four runs with the Gatling guns, then bombs and "mopping up" with napalm. Unloading all of their ordnance because, should they run into difficulty during a mission and be forced to return to base still carrying bombs, ground troops would refuse to stand by with firehoses. Beaucoup VC. Beaucoup body count. The war, the Vietnamese officer accompanying Willson said, would soon be won.

*     *     *

In high school, Brian Willson had dreamed of playing professional baseball. Good enough to attract big-league scouts, he received an offer but decided to attend college, so that he could work for the FBI. In 1964, after graduating from Eastern Baptist College, he enrolled in American University Law School, and taught Sunday school. While attending EBC, he had worked for Barry Goldwater's presidential campaign. One evening at chapel, Willson announced to his fellow students that, to end the war, it just might be necessary to drop a nuclear bomb on North Vietnam. Communism, he told them, had to be stopped once and for all. Godlessness, he continued, had gone far enough.

A short time later, Willson read that the World Council of Churches had condemned the bombing of North Vietnam. Enraged, he told friends that J. Edgar Hoover had been right all along. *They* were everywhere, even in the church, posing as men and women of God but really hard-core pretenders, atheists, devious subverters of our nation's youth. To express their displeasure with the WCC, Willson and his Sunday school students drafted a letter, warning that organization that it had been subverted by "masters of deceit" posing as true Christians.

The war in Vietnam raged on and Willson received his draft notice, joined the Air Force and was later assigned to Operation Safeside, an Air Force unit being created to defend air bases in hostile territory. He was sent to Fort Campbell for twelve weeks' training in patrols, ambushes, and intelligence-gathering. Members of the team learned base combat security, practiced stalking and killing the enemy, were shown how to thrust a bayonet into the soft spots in a Viet Cong's throat, to deftly rip out the enemy's Adam's apple or pluck out his eyes in hand-to-hand combat. When the training was completed, each man was awarded a special ranger patch and issued a blue beret. In March 1969, his unit was shipped to Vietnam to help provide security for Binh Thuy air base in the Mekong Delta. There were 5 six-man fire teams, and two mortar units. Willson was a section leader, a role corresponding to a platoon leader in the army.

Willson was still strongly anti-Communist, but had experienced something deeply troubling and inexplicable during his training for Operation Safeside. What had always seemed like an abstraction, something that one watched in movies or read in comic books, suddenly became real. "Thrust and plunge!" shouted the drill instructor. Not shallow but deep, not slow but fast. You're not playing house with the kiddies on the block, he screamed. You're killing the enemy before *he* kills you. Fair? You'll goddamn think it's fair when you're trying to jerk some gook's bayonet from your own windpipe. Willson balked, stepping back not only physically, but in some way that he could not yet fully understand. *Pussy. Shit-for-brains. Civilian slime.* He balked, refusing to thrust his bayonet into a dummy that he felt would soon be transformed into a living, breathing, Vietnamese. Stalking through the woods, his face coated with greasepaint, he'd discovered that he was not a gung-ho killer after all, something he would later recall as the first great revelation of his life.

The base was attacked frequently, but it was the bodies, a seemingly endless stream of corpses coming in from surrounding areas for shipment to Saigon, that disturbed Willson most. Watching the black rubber bags being heaved onto planes, he could not help thinking that inside were the remains of boys too young to drink or vote back in the States, man-children who, before being taught to kill and dropped into the bush, had scooped the loop in their '65 Chevys on Saturday nights, arms around their skinny girlfriends, radio blaring, adolescents whose mothers still washed and folded their underwear, put away their socks, kept their dinner warm until they got home from football practice. At sock-hops they had danced to the Supremes and Temptations, and dreamed of starting their own rock-and-roll band. Now, they were killers, stalking the rice paddies and mangrove forests until a sniper put a bullet between their eyes or a booby-trap blew them in half. The bags were heavy, slippery in the terrible heat. Sometimes, when they were roughly tossed or dropped, Willson expected to hear a cry or a curse.

On the base, Willson's men worked twenty-four hours a day, with twelve hours off between shifts. When not working they drank heavily and tried to cope with their loneliness and boredom by patronizing prostitutes. Between the officers' club and a bunker was a patio where pornographic films were shown each night. When the Viet Cong launched a mortar attack, everyone would scramble into the bunker until the shelling stopped. Then they would return to the patio, rewind the film, open another beer, and continue watching *Confessions of a Nympho Nurse*.

Willson began to wonder if he were hallucinating. As a boy he had played war, read war comics, and gone to war films, cheering when John Wayne and friends charged enemy positions, shouting with joy when Audie Murphy, the most highly decorated American who served in World War II, slaughtered entire companies of German soldiers. The men in those films were so brave, so cheerful and unaffected by the horrors of warfare (much later he would discover that

Audie Murphy had kept a loaded pistol under his pillow, drank heavily, and suffered from post-traumatic stress syndrome all his life). After a battle they cracked jokes, made love to beautiful women, and spoke like Greek philosophers about the need for men to kill and die for their country in war. Yet most of the men with whom Willson lived and worked in Vietnam kept calendars on which they scratched out each day served, like prisoners waiting for their twelve-month sentence to expire. The grand charges, backed up by Wagnerian orchestras, turned out to be leech-ridden forays into the heart of darkness. Instead of epic monologues on patriotic duty, soldiers cursed the heat, complained about the food, and asked "what the fuck" they were doing in Southeast Asia. When the base was attacked, John Wayne did not rise out of the smoke and debris to lead a squad of cheering riflemen in a counterattack. The mortars fell and the air filled with sudden shrieks of pain and guttural bursts of fear, followed by intervals of terrifying silence.

Willson began to feel that he was living out a nightmare, some insane vision orchestrated by men and women who lived in bubbles of self-delusion, Harvard and Vassar pogues who went home after a day of meetings and memos, phone calls and press conferences, to split-level houses in the suburbs or townhouses in Georgetown, places with pastel walls and polished floors, Persian rugs and tasteful furniture. If they could just spend one day, one mosquito-ravaged 110-degree day in the Delta, looking at and smelling the results of their cocktail prescriptions for the Vietnamese. Just one day in the burn ward of a MASH unit, watching doctors and nurses shooting morphine into things that resembled overcooked chuck roasts more than nineteen-year-old males.

Willson listened to his own thoughts, wondering how on earth he'd ever traveled ten thousand miles to inflict pain on people who, he'd decided, were clearly not his enemy. He wished the war's architects could see, as he had, small boys sitting atop water buffalos at dusk, the setting sun transforming beast and boy into a piece of sculpture; mama-sans stickthin from work and hunger, teeth blackened from betel juice, rocking a child to sleep in the doorway of a thatched hooch; a thousand-year-old farmer slogging knee-deep behind a water buffalo dragging a thousand-year-old plow.

Willson told his commanding officer that he would never again take part in any effort to evaluate the "effectiveness" of South Vietnamese air strikes. Furthermore, he declared, the bombing just had to stop. Willson also sent messages by courier through the chain of command, informing his superiors that he was opposed to free-fire zone bombing, wanted the random killing of women and children to stop, wanted the whole fucking war to end. He forwarded copies of the memorandums to U.S. Senators Javits and Goodell of New York, exhorting them to intervene on behalf of the Vietnamese people.

Brian Willson waited, and the killing continued. In the morning young virile, confident, hard-muscled headhunters slid into the bush, returning hours or days later as stiff, torn, mud-covered relics from the museum of horrors. Planes took off, returned with their Gatling guns and bomb-bay areas empty. Bodies arrived, were hosed down, pieced back together, embalmed, packed and shipped home to be buried in some smalltown cemetery on the other side of the universe. One day, a telegram arrived ordering Lt. Willson to pack up and get out of the Republic of South Vietnam. Apparently the Air Force had decided that the war would be won without malcontents and subversives like him.

Willson was reassigned to a base in Louisiana, and charged with a number of counts related to his opposition to the war. His movements were closely monitored by the Office of Special Investigations whose agents frequently interviewed Captain Willson (ironically, he was promoted following his attenuated tour of duty with Operation Safeside) and the men under his command about his "anti-war activities." Brian allowed his hair to grow longer than military standards permitted at the time, lived off-base, taught a course at the local Unitarian church on U.S. involvement in Vietnam, and drove to work each morning in a "flower-mobile," a Volkswagen Beetle that resembled a float in the Rose Bowl parade. Furious, the base commander tried to ban Willson's "hippie machine," but agreed to a compromise. The car could be driven to and from base, but the guards at the gate would not salute its driver.

Willson agreed to the compromise because, like hundreds of thousands of men and women returning from the war, he wanted only to be left alone, to complete his tour and leave the military and the war behind. For Willson, Vietnam had been a twilight zone out of which he had emerged, if not a new person then changed in some profound and irrevocable way. His belief system had been turned upside down, shattered, dissolved, leaving him with a kind of nagging bitterness that occasionally erupted into rage. Everything he'd ever believed to be sacred, everything he'd ever thought was inviolable, had turned to dust. He felt eviscerated, scooped out by the myriad lies that had informed his vision, inspired him to act, given him some tangible sense of well-being and worth.

In 1970, as Richard Nixon was preparing to invade Cambodia, Brian Willson was honorably separated from the U.S. Air Force. After two more years of inactive duty, he was honorably discharged. He had returned to law school, graduated but never really practiced a profession that reflected, in some very obvious ways, the homicidal games Henry Kissinger and friends were playing in Chile and Guatemala, Laos, Cambodia, and Vietnam. Brian worked at prison reform for a time, then tried his hand at farming, no longer surprised as year after year the killing abroad continued, the divisions at home deepened. Then, one evening in April, the news showed panicky South Vietnamese soldiers kicking and shooting their way onto evacuation planes out of Danang, crowds of civilians desperately trying to board helicopters lifting from the roof of the American Embassy in Saigon, a plane filled with Vietnamese children crashing and burning at Ton Son Nhut airport. The lying, Willson thought, was at least over. The war, for Vietnam veterans and the Vietnamese people, was not.

Willson later took a job as director of a Vietnam veterans outreach center in Greenfield, Massachusetts, one of the self-help storefront centers the state legislature had agreed to fund. He sat under bridges and walked the streets with homeless Vietnam veterans, listening to stories so terrible that, even though he knew they were true, he struggled against believing. Tales told, it seemed, by men who somehow had managed to crawl out of those black sweaty bags at Binh Thuy, walk away from death and now were standing like specters on the nation's streetcorners, calling out to a world that wished to deny not only their deaths, but that they had ever been alive. Drugs, alcohol, suicides. During the period Willson worked at the vets center, twelve veterans went down by their own hand, another thirty or forty tried to kill themselves and failed. Willson visited with "bush vets," (those who were psychologically still in the Vietnam jungle), signed young men in and out of mental hospitals and detoxification programs, listened and quite often cried late into the night, the sun rising like an exhausted and bewildered witness to some unfathomable crime.

Through reading and talking to veterans of other wars, Willson discovered that this was not the first time the U.S. government had sent young boys off to battle with trumpets and cheers, only to ignore or mistreat them when they returned home. For example, as the Great Depression of the 1930s deepened, men who had fought in the trenches during World War I were reduced to begging in the streets to keep from starving. Many had been given government bonus certificates by the federal government, which they could turn in for money after several years. But the veterans were desperate. They'd lost their homes and their farms. There were no jobs, no food stamps, no public assistance. Their children were starving, dying from a host of illnesses caused by malnutrition. In the summer of 1932, twenty thousand World War I veterans walked, hitchhiked, drove battered cars and rode freight trains into Washington, D.C. They built lean-tos out of old newspapers, packing crates, cardboard boxes and tarpaper, and they waited to be paid their bonus. The House of Representatives passed a bill agreeing to pay the veterans, but the bill lost in the Senate. President Hoover ordered the army to evict the demonstrators and, led by General Douglas

MacArthur, Major Dwight Eisenhower, and George S. Patton, battle-dressed troops marched into the veterans' encampment, ripping down and burning their shacks, teargassing their families, shooting two veterans to death, and driving the rest out of the nation's capital.

Civil War veterans, according to author Hamlin Garland, had also been met with indifference and even hostility when they returned from the battlefield. In his short story, "The Return Of A Private," Hamlin describes how Private Smith and a few survivors from the Civil War returned to Wisconsin, only to discover that while they were gone the country had lost interest in them:

> Three of them were gaunt and brown, the fourth was gaunt and pale, with signs of fever and ague upon him. One had a great scar down his temple, one limped, and they all had unnaturally large, bright eyes, showing emaciation. There were no hands greeting them at the station, no banks of gayly dressed ladies waving handkerchiefs and shouting 'Bravo!' as they came in on a caboose of a freight train into the towns that had cheered and blared at them on their way to war. As they looked out or stepped upon the platform for a moment, while the train stood at the station, the loafers looked at them indifferently. Their blue coats, dusty and grimy, were too familiar now to excite notice, much less a friendly word. They were the last of the army to return, and the loafers were surfeited with such sights.[1]

The men returned home to discover that while they were gone the "millionaires had been sending their money to England for safe keeping," and their own farms were so heavily mortgaged that it would take a lifetime of Herculean work to redeem them. "The common soldier of the American volunteer army," concludes the narrator, "had returned. His war with the South was over, and his fight, his daily running fight with nature and against the injustice of his fellowmen, was begun again."[2]

And there was Ernest Hemingway's masterpiece, "Soldier's Home," in which a soldier returning from the great battles at Belleau Wood, Soissons, the Champagne, and St. Mihiel, wants to talk about his experiences, but finds that no one really wants to listen. To be listened to at all, the soldier discovers, he must lie, embellish, indulge the fantasies of his listeners. He must never talk about what really happened, that he, the brave soldier, had been "badly, sickeningly frightened all the time . . ."[3]

Brian Willson's goal was to help Vietnam veterans avoid becoming victims of society and their own self-pity. In order for the nation to heal its wounds, he argued, Americans had to be willing to hear the veterans' stories. But it was difficult for the men with whom Wilson worked to talk to anyone who had not been in the snake-infested swamps, who hadn't wept with terror during an ambush in the Ia Drang Valley, or screamed in primal rage during a firefight in the Central Highlands of Vietnam. People who hadn't been there, veterans would tell Wilson, could never hope to understand. People who hadn't smelled burning flesh, hadn't felt their bladder contract until it leaked during a night ambush or watched their best friend ascend, in pieces, into the triple-canopied jungle, could not hope to know. Besides, the nation wanted to hear traditional war stories, not tales of pure horror. Americans wanted to hear the old myths retold, to believe, like warrior societies always had, that through killing the warrior helped regenerate his culture. They wanted to believe there were still heroes who, through war and killing, could immortalize the society. People wanted to be titillated by tales of bravery, not told the truth about free-fire zones, turned on by guts and glory, not told about young boys crying for their mothers as the North Vietnamese went up and down the line of wounded, shooting each one in the head. Brian Willson wanted his fellow veterans to tell their stories because he knew just how badly people wanted not to believe what had really happened in Vietnam. And because, like the Berrigans whom he greatly admired, he believed in the liberating power of "truth-telling." There would be consequences, of course, for telling the truth, but the consequences of remaining silent were far worse.

Under the auspices of the Veterans Education Project, Willson tried to warn high school students that they might soon find themselves in the jungles of El Salvador, Nicaragua, or elsewhere, forced to choose between shooting civilians or being charged with insubordination, killing or being killed by children, following the military's orders or the dictates of their own conscience. Would they be willing to drop napalm (manufactured by "we let you do great things" Dow Chemical) on women and children? Could they stand by and watch people their own age rolling and screaming as they tried to put out their burning flesh?

Surveying the wide-eyed students in a classroom or auditorium, Willson would invariably be struck by how young, clean, honest, really decent these young faces were. And sadly, how misinformed. Gullible. Deceived. Misled. Lied to. Kept in the dark. Primed for slaughter. He had seen their history and political science texts, one or two paragraphs stating that Vietnam was just another war, a mistake, an un-

fortunate episode in our nation's exemplary past, an histor-
ical aberration better left to gather dust, unnoticed.

"Think about what you're doing!" he would urge his
youthful audience. "Don't just sit there! Question authority!" Don't believe what they are telling you. It's the same
unadulterated bullshit they fed my generation for breakfast,
lunch, and dinner, the same rhetorical rubbish, the exact formula for a free trip to the twilight zone, a one-way ticket to
insanity, wounds that will never heal, shattered limbs and
psyches that stay that way, even though it appears, on the
surface, that our technological genius has figured out a way
to mend them, put the pieces so neatly back together.

Discouraged by Vietnam veteran Senator John Kerry's
criticism of the Sandinistas, Willson left with a group of
North Americans, including Vietnam veterans, for a fact-
finding tour of Nicaragua. The group walked roads regularly
mined by the Contras and observed the devastating results
of their attacks on the Nicaraguan economy and people.
Near Esteli, during an earlier trip Willson had made to Nicaragua, the Contras had attacked a series of cooperatives. For
three nights had he listened to the mortars and watched
tracers crisscrossing the sky. Bodies were carried in—five
mothers and two children. Wilson felt, once again, a bloody
*deja vu*, the rage rising, his heart pounding like the mortars
outside, words trying to form something articulate out of this
slaughter.

"Mother," said Willson, turning to a Nicaraguan woman
who was giving him shelter, "You know I've seen this before
in Vietnam. And I promise you now, I will do everything in
my power to stop this killing from continuing." He had no
idea what he really meant, only that his words were not rhetorical. Instead of feeling depressed, he felt empowered.

Standing in that impoverished living room, watching the bodies being carried in, hearing the gunfire and seeing the tracers, Willson vividly remembered napalmed Vietnamese women and children. The woman hugging him was sixty-five. She had raised eleven children in a hut with a dirt floor and a few pots and pans. One of her sons had been killed by the Contras. She thought Wilson was afraid, unable to understand fully when he told her in his broken Spanish that he was in solidarity with her. She hugged him tighter. "No!" he shouted. "I'm not afraid. I'm just furious. Furious!"

Willson began to read about the ancient tradition of peace warriors who would never maim or kill, choosing, if faced with a relentless adversary, to accept injury or death before harming another human being. Nicaragua had been a veritable looking glass of schizophrenic rhetoric: destroy the village to save it, kill the child to keep it from growing up to be a Communist, all of it was nicely frosted over with Manifest Destiny rhetoric and noblesse oblige. Now, he felt his own center shifting, the fears that had kept him stuck—financial insecurity, social approbation, prison, death—lifting like great water birds, slowly but with true grace turning to mere specks on the horizon. For the first time in his life, Brian Willson felt almost free of fear.

Willson began organizing Veterans Peace Action Teams to rebuild what the Contras had destroyed. In Nicaraguan hospital wards he visited amputees and spoke with the wounded and maimed. Looking into the eyes of a man whose legs had been blown off by a U.S. landmine, Willson said that he was personally sorry for what his country had done in Nicaragua, sorry, ashamed, and angry. "I commend you for your courage," Willson told the wounded patients. "You inspire me to do more."

They replied that Willson was not to blame for their injuries. "We hold your government responsible, not you," they said. "It's not you, not the American people who are killing us. It's your government."

"*No*," Willson replied, shaking with anger, "I *am* part of our government that kills and maims in our name. We, the people, must take responsibility." All over Nicaragua, people said the same thing, and always Willson replied that he respected their views but could not fully accept their kindness. People who did nothing to stop the killing, Willson said, were reneging on their responsibility as citizens. People who paid their taxes, kept quiet, and accepted the homicidal foreign policies of the Reagan administration were complicit with murder, accomplices to the terrorizing of the Nicaraguan people.

In Nicaragua, Willson met Charles Liteky, Medal of Honor winner and veteran of two tours of duty in Vietnam. Like others who had witnessed the Contra's attacks on civilians, Liteky was shaken and angered. "All these years," he told Willson, "I've been duped. You know, I always thought I believed in the just war' theory, but this isn't war down here. This is murder. Cold-blooded, first-degree homicide."

Returning to the states, Liteky and Willson, along with other veterans, organized a fast on the steps of the U.S. Capitol to stop Contra aid. The stakes, they realized, were very high. Many had tried to prevail on Mr. Reagan and Congress to stop the killing. All had failed. Willson and his friends wanted to express not only their frustration with U.S. policies, but their respect for human life. Their fast, they would tell supporters, was not just against something or someone, but *for* the courageous people in Nicaragua, *for* life over death, peace instead of war, friendship instead of hatred and animosity. After forty-seven days on a water-only diet, Vietnam veteran George Miso, a victim of Agent Orange poisoning, lost a considerable amount of weight and was at risk of becoming seriously, perhaps even fatally, ill. Willson fasted for thirty-six days, Duncan Murphy for thirty-three, and Charles Liteky for forty-seven days. The President did not pay them a visit. Congress did not invite them inside to speak. And the killing in Nicaragua continued, though the fast had made the statement they wished to make.

In California, Brian Willson helped organize the Nuremberg actions at Concord Naval Weapons station, the largest weapons depot on the West Coast. From Concord, weapons are moved by train and truck to ships anchored in the harbor about three miles away, then sent to El Salvador where they are distributed to government troops. On June 10, 1987, Willson and a small number of friends from veterans' and religious communities in the San Francisco area began a sustained vigil outside Concord. Day after day they stood alongside the tracks holding signs:

REMEMBER NUREMBERG

STOP THE WAR IN CENTRAL AMERICA

STOP THE KILLING

Some of the signs were painted with crosses or the names of people who had been murdered in Nicaragua and El Salvador.

To prepare for their planned blockade of the weapons depot on September 1, 1987, Brian and friends wrote to the base commander, the local police, and many congressmen, explaining exactly what they were planning to do, where they were going to do it, and why. They would sit on the tracks, waiting for and stopping the munitions train. In the spirit of nonviolence, they wished to be open rather than secretive about their actions, loving rather than hateful.

As September approached, word of the impending blockade spread through the community. A local newspaper quoted the demonstrators as stating, "We plan to block the trains on Tuesday morning by being on the tracks." Rumors flew. Gossip spread. The commander of the base sent cables to the head of the Navy in Washington, D.C., warning that Brian Willson would not move off the tracks. He is a Vietnam veteran, wrote the commander, has fasted on the steps of the Capitol and should be taken seriously. Local officials would be notified, and they would be prepared to arrest him. But there would also be other veterans on the tracks, a sustained campaign of civil disobedience and undoubtedly more demonstrations and arrests.

September 1, 1987. 10:00 A.M. Forty people gathered on the tracks, singing, reading passages from Gandhi, Martin Luther King, Jr., and the Bible. Five newspaper reporters milled about, writing in pocket-size notebooks. There were no television crews, the sky was a wonderful pale blue, and the sun flashed playfully in and out of an occasional cloud. At 11:30, the vigil formally began, when the group sent a delegation to the main gate to announce that trains leaving from the weapons station would now be blocked. Willson signed a letter stating the group's intentions, and the duty officer at the gate stamped it with the time, 11:45. Within moments, the first train, laden with weapons and explosives, commenced to roll out of the station, but stopped, curiously, for ten minutes at the main gate.

World War II veteran Duncan Murphy, and David Duncombe, veteran of World War II and Korea, and Brian Willson placed themselves on the tracks, waiting to be arrested. Behind them, one on each side of the tracks, demonstrators supported an enormous banner that read: NUREMBERG ACTIONS. A squad of Marines wearing flak jackets and carrying M-16s at port-arms arrived. During summer months when other demonstrations were held, sheriff's department and highway patrol units were invariably waiting for the protesters, but now there were no squad cars or walkie-talkies, no uniformed police at all. The Marines stood within thirty or forty feet of the demonstrators.

At approximately noon the train chugged once, twice, three times, and moved asthmatically through the main gate. It would come close, perhaps even nudge them, then stop. When it did, the demonstrators would be removed from the tracks, hands pulled behind their backs and wrists lashed together with thin strips of black plastic.

The train moved forward. There was no gate blocking the highway over which it must cross, and the train was not escorted by the police or military. A red light beside the highway was flashing and clanging, and the train was accelerating. Brian's wife, who was standing in front of her husband, was waving frantically, screaming at the engineer to stop. Two men (later Brian would discover they were Vietnam veterans) standing on the front of the locomotive shook their heads. Negative. The train roared, whistle blowing, drowning out all warnings. Negative, no way. David Duncombe dove for cover, landing on his side, rolling clear. Duncan Murphy leaped high as if for the winning basket down the chute, landing on the railing of the cow catcher. Willson tried to rise from a sitting position with his right hand on the tracks, but the train, moving at three times its normal speed, smashed into his face, rolling him backward, dragging him under the wheels, breaking his skull, and shredding his legs just below the knees. The train moved on, leaving a bloody, mutilated bundle on the tracks.

Brian Willson's wife, Holly, bent over her husband, wrapping her left arm under his shoulders and cradling his shattered head. Friends wept and screamed for help, moving like underwater divers in slow-motion shock. A Navy ambulance waiting nearby refused to aid Willson. Five minutes passed. No help arrived. Blood flowed from Willson's mangled legs and head wounds, exposing his brain. Holly and friends tried to stem the flow. Another five minutes, and the Marines took no action. At last, a civilian ambulance arrived to take Brian to a hospital. One of his legs had been severed by the train. Attending physicians told Willson's wife they could not save the other leg; it would have to be amputated.

"No, I wouldn't call it an accident," Willson says, politely but firmly, "Because it wasn't. I call it a frontal assault. I mean, there was six hundred feet of clear visibility, and those two guys my wife were calling to, who are Vietnam veterans incidentally, were supposed to see that the tracks were clear. That's their job, because that train is loaded with bombs and bullets and they just can't afford to have an accident. Besides, if they really believed we were terrorists, I suppose they might imagine we would strap bombs to our bodies."

"I mean, you really don't know what you're going to do when the train is about to run you down. Jump, roll, sit there? Our commitment was not to leave the tracks, but something, some instinctive thing takes over. Duncan Murphy, who remembers everything that happened, says, 'There was just no way I was going to leave those tracks.' We were committed to stopping a train that was going to murder innocent people. And that was the least we could do to be on those tracks, just to get that death train to stop, even if only for ten minutes.

"Oh, I know what the Navy says, that I was negligent, suicidal, crazy, or have an unstable background, and therefore they are exonerated. That'll be their case."

If the attempt on his life was meant to stifle nonviolent resistance to sending munitions to military and death squads in El Salvador, it has failed, says Willson. Ever since the September action, demonstrators have sat near or been on the tracks twenty-four hours a day. When the train does move it travels at only one mile an hour, with a Marine guard walking in front and a contingent of military personnel and police prepared to arrest any demonstrators.

"No," Willson says, "I'm not afraid to go back to Concord. I don't intend to stop protesting. I feel even more empowered. I mean, what are they going to do now, send me to 'Nam? They've taken my legs, tried to kill me. So they can send me to jail, do whatever they want, whatever they choose to do, but I want to make sure that I do what I feel in my heart is the right thing. And what I think others want us to do. Just let me read you a letter I received from Patti Davis, President Reagan's daughter, while I was in the hospital:

> For the past few years, I've listened with growing dismay to my father's aggressive and anti-Sandinista rhetoric, and his absurd references to the contras as

freedom fighters. But nothing I have felt over these years equals the sickness in my heart over what has happened to you. It symbolizes everything that is wrong and unjust in this country. I can only hope that this tragedy will not take from you the faith and commitment that led you to those tracks in the first place. I'm sure you sat down with the confidence that you would walk away from that confrontation, and onto another and another, until your message was heard. But you will walk again. All of us who have prayed and shed tears for you will be your legs.

Early evening and few cars on the highway, valleys stretching out like long black thumbs, billowy grey clouds bouncing silently—perhaps we just can't hear them—off one another. Silver shafts, the road lifting, an endless shimmer, puddles of gold among the wheat and corn, shrinking, expanding, sucked dry by some mysterious, avaricious force.

Darkness and scattered stars, a desultory half-moon. By the time I reach home the children are asleep, the house creaking like an old sloop anchored in storm. Rain tacktacking on the roof, the shutters squeaking. The video shows Brain Willson and a squad of Vietnam veterans walking down a dusty road in Nicaragua. A woman passes by, barefoot and carrying an umbrella to deflect the afternoon sun. Wide-eyed with curiosity, children watch the North Americans pass by. But why, a reporter asks, are Wilson and his friends walking in the most dangerous section of Nicaragua? Why are they risking their lives? "We're walking against fear," replies Willson, smiling. But, the reporter insists, there's a war going on. "Yeah, but only one country is at war with Nicaragua, and that's my own," says Willson. Cut to smoke. The Contras staging an ambush a mile or two away. Sandinista troops racing by. Shouts. A burning vehicle, and a wounded man screaming in pain.

"No," Willson declares. "We do not plan on turning back." The men, and two women, continue walking.

# Notes

1. Hamlin Garland, "The Return Of A Private" quoted in A. Walton Litz, ed., *Major American Short Stories* (New York: Oxford, 1980), 314.

2. Ibid., 328.

3. Ernest Hemingway, *In Our Time* (New York: Scribners, 1930), 91.

# Six

---

## *Protests and Prayers: The Story of an Irish-American Family*

---

My heart is moved by all I cannot save:
so much has been destroyed

I have to cast my lot with those
who age after age, perversely,

with no extraordinary power,
reconstitute the world

ADRIENNE RICH

Teresa Grady's grandparents left Ireland during the great potato famine, fleeing starvation and British tyranny. Yet painful as it may have been, they never forgot their Irish heritage. They had known the dreaded sound of the bailiff's knock and suffered a hunger so deep that food could not make it go away—a hunger that would linger with a thousand bitter memories, handed down generation after generation like family heirlooms. In this sense, Teresa's grandparents were no different than many other Irish immigrants. Indeed, Irish folklore is replete with stories and songs about people fighting and dying for justice, like Molly Maguire, a kind of mid-nineteenth-century Irish Robin Hood who carried two pistols under her red petticoat, and used her guns to drive off landlords and bailiffs whenever they attempted to evict tenants. So effective were Molly's assassinations that, according to legend, parts of Ireland were inhabited only by her own followers. In the U.S., Irish coal miners who fought for decent working conditions in the hills of Pennsylvania in the late nineteenth century were dubbed "Molly Maguires" by a reporter hostile to their cause. The "Mollys" were spied on, beaten, and murdered by agents working for the coal companies. In June 1877, ten of their members were hanged for crimes that, even as they were taken to the scaffold, they denied committing. The primary witness at their trials was an informer and gunman who worked for one of the most virulent anti-union mine owners. Similarly, a century later an informer would turn in Teresa Grady's husband to the FBI, claiming that he intended to use violence in his efforts to end the Vietnam War.

Teresa attended Catholic primary and secondary schools, and a women's Catholic college, joining Catholic action groups like the Young Christian Student organization, and later the Young Christian Workers. At an engagement party for mutual friends, she met John Grady, recently returned from studying at the London School of Economics. She was third-generation, John second-generation Irish. His parents had immigrated from County Galway, his mother a maid, his father laboring on the railroad. As a boy he had grown up on stories about Irish peasants being exploited by landlords and jailed by a government of occupation. But it was most exciting to learn how some people had fought back, knowing they couldn't win, certain that when caught they would be imprisoned or executed. For centuries, men and women had risked their lives not for something so grand as "freedom," but for the basic right to feed their children, have a home, live with a modicum of security and dignity in their own country.

John introduced Teresa to the writings of Irish patriot and socialist James Connolly. On their bookshelves, like dog-eared twins, stood the same texts. In their hearts, the same passions: to live in a world where a man or woman is not judged by the color of his or her skin, a world where the church really means it when it declares "Thou Shalt Not Kill," and where disputes can be settled with words rather than bullets.

With a master's degree in sociology from Fordham, a charming smile, and an extraordinary gift for conversation, John Grady might easily have climbed the corporate ladder, settling with his wife and children into some comfortable corner of 'fifties ennui. Instead, he took a low-paying job with *Jubilee* magazine. He met and became a great admirer of Dorothy Day and Thomas Merton, was introduced to and became lifelong friends with Philip and Daniel Berrigan, and began writing about and working with people who were trying to redefine what it meant to be a Christian in a racist and militaristic culture.

In the late 'fifties and early 'sixties, new possibilities for social justice were fomenting in the church, the social sciences, and in various parts of the world. John and Teresa felt these developments were exciting and found them to be personally nourishing. Many of these ideas were expressed in the social encyclicals, such as *Rerum Novarum*, and in the Second Vatican Council, "The Church in the Modern World." They could also be found in publications like the

*Catholic Worker, Jubilee, Commonweal, America,* and *Sign* magazine. Through the Catholic Worker Movement, the Young Christian Worker Movement, and the Priest Worker Movement, new ideas and possibilities for social justice were translated into action. The new ideas were also nourished by and celebrated in the Liturgical Movement. During these years John and Teresa were encouraged and inspired by liturgist/activist Monsignor R. Hillenbrand of Chicago, Teresa's pastor; liturgist J. G. Kealy; sociologist Father Joe Fitzpatrick S.J. of Fordham University; Dorothy Dohern of *Integrity* magazine; Dorothy Day; Peter Maurin; Ammon Hennacy, and many others.

They shared Daniel and Philip Berrigan's admiration for the courage and dedication of the French worker priests, many of whom had been members of the French resistance, risking execution and prison to defy the German occupation. The worker priests were profoundly anti-colonial and anti-imperialistic, their ideas grounded in the communitarian and pacifist philosophy of the early, pre-Constantine, Christians. John and Teresa were also attracted to the works of Simone Weil, a French philosopher and writer Charles De Gaulle had dismissed as a madwoman. In one of her essays, written before she died in England on August 24, 1943, Weil developed a theme that would be reiterated four decades later in the writings and during the court appearances of Plowshare activists. A careful examination of war, Weil argued, reveals that the killing and dying have no rationally definable objective. Wars are fought not to resolve reasonable conflicts, but to perpetuate myths and collective fantasies. "What is called national security," wrote Weil, "is a chimerical state of things in which one would keep for oneself alone the power to make war while all other countries would be unable to do so . . . War is therefore made in order to keep or increase the means of making war. All international politics revolve in this vicious circle. . . . But, why must one be able to make war? This no one knows any more than the Trojans knew why they had to keep Helen.[1]

For a time, John and Teresa worked with author and scholar Ivan Illyich in Puerto Rico, a country suffering from the "benevolent exploitation" which had begun in 1898 when the U.S. paid Spain $20 million to add Guam, Puerto Rico, and the Philippines to its empire. The Gradys worked to bring U.S. citizens to the island for what they called "mission vacations." Instead of staying in American-owned hotels, visitors lived with Puerto Rican families, getting to know and becoming friends with their hosts, observing and studying first-hand the devastating effects of imperialism on Puerto Rico's economy and social structure. Many U.S. companies hired only women because they were the cheapest source of labor, forcing husbands to remain at home and, because of their culture's centuries-old value system, to feel deeply humiliated. Puerto Rican society, visitors who returned from these mission vacations would tell friends, was under economic, political, and social siege by the U.S.-owned multi-national corporations.

When they were married, John and Teresa had inscribed *"Through Him, With Him, In Him"* on their wedding bands. Faith and the Catholic church would be a part of their commitment to one another, a grounding point, inextricable from their Irish roots and deep sense of family and community. To many of their fellow Irish-Americans and Catholics, the Gradys' passionate belief in racial equality was sheer stupidity, their opposition to war utopian nonsense, and their willingness to challenge the church pure arrogance, if not a form of heresy. Catholics, conventional wisdom seemed to dictate, should be seen, not heard; should obey, not question; follow, not lead; go to war when called to do so, kill and die when the state and church said one must.

As a young man studying labor at the London School of Economics, John had experienced racism and discrimination first hand. He was proud, sometimes extravagantly so, of his Irish heritage. Yes, he would explain, he was an American, but his family's roots were in those Celtic stone walls and houses, built by master craftsmen, stone on stone without a trace of mortar; magic, moss-covered, rainbow-spouting walls. His family's traditions stemmed from those tiny fishing villages where the odor of burning turf mingled with lamb stew on a Sunday morning, and later, after Mass, there would surely be a pint of stout in Murphy's pub, some good "crack" (conversation), a nap in the afternoon, and a bit of music later in the evening.

"Bogmen" and "Little People," his fellow students scoffed. Lazy to their marrow, dreamers and schemers, drunkards, brawlers, and bums. Such language Grady had heard before, but not about his own people. And never had he felt the sting, the true harm of it, the way such comments can gnaw like acid at a person's self-esteem, leaving one feeling bewildered, hurt, and bitter. He had experienced something that few white Americans ever had or would, a discovery for which he felt very grateful; he had found out how it felt to be black in a racist culture.

In the early 'sixties, John opened a Montessori school in Harlem, busing black children out to New Rochelle and white children in to the ghetto. He wanted his own children to do more than sympathize with oppressed people on some intellectual level or commiserate with the poor from a comfortable, suburban distance. He wished for them to understand not only the sociological and political roots of racism in the United States, but to grasp in some deeper sense what it means to experience fear, animosity, and discrimination—things blacks and chicanos are forced to face every day of their lives.

As the war in Southeast Asia escalated, John and Teresa attended church less often, choosing instead to celebrate Mass at "alternative" liturgies; to worship, they would tell friends, the God of peace rather than the gods of metal. Sometimes, in her exasperation with the church's lack of response to the Vietnam War, Teresa would insist that her parish priest acknowledge that the war was taking a terrible toll both on the Vietnamese and Americans. A toll that could be measured not only by the number of dead and wounded, but in the terrible divisions Vietnam was causing within the church and the nation. Did church officials not realize that young Catholic boys were being taught to hate, not love; to destroy, not preserve human life? How on earth could priests talk about forgiveness and loving one's enemies on Sunday, only to approve of mass murder on Monday? During the Prayers of the Faithful, Teresa would sometimes add a prayer of petition for those suffering the ravages of war, especially the children. At other times she asked for enlightenment of our leaders, so they might bring about peace. She was an indefatigable leafleteer after Mass, and worked with peace and justice committees to educate people about the war through films and speaker programs.

On February 21, 1970, Secretary of State Henry Kissinger met secretly for the first time with North Vietnamese negotiator Le Duc Tho, hoping to find a way to end U.S. involvement in the war and, simultaneously, "save face." Three months later, Richard M. Nixon informed the nation that

U.S. forces had invaded Cambodia. (This was the first public acknowledgment of such an incursion; however, combat veterans who served in Southeast Asia say they ran missions into Cambodia long before this.) Once again the President asked that the nation be patient, trust its leadership, believe that expanding the war was really the best way to end it. On May 4, 1970, members of the Ohio National Guard fired on students at Kent State University, killing four, wounding several others. Mr. Nixon called the protesters "bums."

That government officials would publicly profess their desire for peace while secretly making plans to invade another country did not surprise John Grady. Long before U.S. troops entered Cambodia he had given up any hope that the President and his coterie would tell the American people the truth. Lying and deceit among government officials had been elevated to new Machiavellian heights during the past few years. In courtrooms, during the trials of the Berrigans and others, he had heard lawyers and prosecutors skillfully deny the truth. He had listened to radio and television newscasters quote the fabrications of White House and Pentagon spokespersons. In the major newspapers he had read the same, unexpurgated, quotes.

In late August 1971, John Grady appeared in a federal courtroom in Camden, New Jersey, chained hand and foot with 27 other protesters who had taken a stand at the Camden draft board. His manacle scraping in the hallway, and the soft popping of news cameras could be heard before they arrived, and so could singing, distant at first, then louder and cheerfully raucous:

> *Oh! then tell me, Sean O'Farrell, where the*
> *gathering is to be?*

> *In the old spot by the river, right well known to*
> *you and me.*
> *One word more—for signal token—whistle up*
> *the marching tune,*
> *With your pike upon your shoulder, by the*
> *rising of the moon.*

The Grady children sat straight in their chairs, hearing
their father's voice strong among the others; emerging, re-
assuring, without a trace of fear. Crisp and clear. An apple
sliced with a clean sharp knife. A window thrown open in
April, a cardinal serenading its mate. Louder.

> *Out from many a mudwall cabin eyes were*
> *watching through the night,*
> *Many a manly breast was throbbing for the*
> *blessed warning light,*
> *Murmurs passed along the valley like the*
> *banshee's lonely croons,*
> *And a thousand blades were flashing at the*
> *rising of the moon.*
> *And, hurrah, my boys, for freedom! 'tis the*
> *rising of the moon.*[2]

The defendants would declare that they were singing for
the burning children. For the Vietnamese the U.S. was destroying, God help us, in order to save them. In the front
row John Grady's children watched and listened as the
charges, adding up like usury, were announced. Their father
and his friends, said those who disagreed with the action
John Grady and the others had taken in Camden, were sab-
oteurs of the social order; conspirators against the ship of
state; a menace to the social fabric; burglars; terrorists; mem-

glars; terrorists; members of the dreamers and schemers club; Catholic revisionists; anti-war crackpots.

The children listened, whispering, staring, trying not to point. In their chains, the defendants smiled, tried to wave, the event more like a soccer match than the beginning of a trial that could send them to prison for forty-five years. "Judge," one of the defendants declared, "I'll call you 'Your Honor,' when you call me, 'Your Honor.'" And the spectators loved it. Optimism in the presence of sanctified despair. Joy in the grip of chains. A rousing good song as the hangman prepares to knot the rope. Like previous trials of anti-war activists, a chance to turn the tables, placing the government itself on trial for its crimes against humanity.

Before the trial, in the streets outside and in the hallways of John Grady's apartment building, agents from the FBI had skulked and prowled, knocking on doors and stopping children, squinting through tinted windows (one easy way to tell it was a 'bureau' car), whispering into radios held in clenched fists: "Where is that Grady bastard? Where?" Seeing these strange men—loaded guns concealed behind their grey trenchcoats, feet tucked into high top Converse sneakers, voices menacingly sweet, so very exotic and obvious—always made the neighborhood children laugh. "Oh look," one young girl quipped, pointing and giggling, "Here comes the Feminine . . . Body . . . Inspectors . . . again." Subpoenaed to testify in the trials of other draft board invaders, John Grady had refused, then disappeared into the underground network that protected the Berrigans and friends.

Sometimes, while their father was underground, the Grady children would be picked up from school and driven in what seemed like circles, looking for some spot where the men in the raincoats and sneakers would not appear, some place where the family could be free to meet and hug John, hear the gentle lilt of his voice. It all seemed like an elaborate game of hide and seek, and the children wanted so badly to tell their friends about their father, to express their pride in him, their belief that what he and the others had done was more than right, it was *just*. The family traveled under assumed names, camping out near Camden, New Jersey, where John Jr. made friends with the camp owner's son, but stuttered and mumbled when asked his own name. He had wanted to shout, to tell his new friends how his father, John Grady, Sr., was trying to stop the war in Vietnam, something all Catholics, all Christians should be doing. "What's your name?" the children teased.

"John," he answered.

"John what?" He hesitated, confused. The children laughed.

Two days later, on the news rack in the campground's grocery store, front-page headlines declared John Grady's capture, and there were photographs of him and friends in handcuffs. John Jr. stared at his father's face. Now, at last, he could tell everyone his real name. Grady it is, and yes, that was his dad all right, and no, John, Jr., did not feel embarrassed or sad. He was not frightened or depressed. No, he didn't need a social worker to help him cope or psychiatrist to probe his psyche. He knew his father and friends might go to prison, but they had stood up for what they believed in. John and his sisters understood: In a land that idolized war, their father and mother had always told them, prison is the price one must pay for working for peace.

Week after week, month after month, the trial of the Camden 28 and the war in Vietnam dragged on. The defendants sat together at several tables, speaking from a podium arranged to face the jury rather than the judge. Each day they announced someone's birthday, the anniversary of some landmark effort to end the killing in Vietnam; drive the British from Ireland; or secure the rights of black Americans to work, worship, and live where they pleased. When the court adjourned for another day, the Grady children would rush forward, swinging on the judge's and jurors' chairs, celebrating another day of hope.

Howard Zinn, author and professor of history at Boston University, explained that our interests in Vietnam were economic, our goal being to secure that country's vast deposits of tin, copper, rubber, and oil. A former employee of the Selective Service explained how the poor, particularly minorities, were being drafted and sent into combat while the rich were bribing their way out of the military. "Were you to do another action like this one," he told the defendants, "I would surely join you." A Gold Star mother, one of her sons sitting at the defendants' table, another killed in Vietnam, praised not the war but the men and women who were working to end the fighting in Southeast Asia. She wept at the thought that some members of Congress and at least three U.S. Presidents had lied to her family and the nation about our intentions in Vietnam.

The trial continued for four months. Since the conclusion of the Catonsville Nine trial, tens of thousands more young men had fled to Canada or Sweden, gone AWOL from the military, or were in prison. Nearly thirty thousand more Americans and hundreds of thousands of Vietnamese had been killed since Richard Nixon declared he had the key, the formula, the *real* light at the end of the tunnel. John Grady and friends asked the jury to act as the conscience of the community, to end the war in their own hearts and help end it for the Vietnamese and our own tortured nation. They could do this, the defendants said, by applying a noble and perfectly legal principle called jury nullification (see page 113).

One of the defendants, Father Edward J. McGowan, S.J., told the court about reading the morning papers before commencing to teach a sophomore history class in Rochester, New York. The year was 1965, and the papers "had mentioned another day of bombing in Vietnam, and the American fleet in the Caribbean was heading towards a tiny country called the Dominican Republic. President Johnson, newly inaugurated, had campaigned on responsible policy toward Southeast Asia, and he was elected overwhelmingly against Barry Goldwater. With all that he started bombing in South Vietnam in February, and troop call-ups were a daily occurrence. It came in a flash. Looking over the thirty-five or so fifteen-year-old boys before me, war was in their future and death and injury and brutality, confusion, alienation, rejection. There had to be a damn good reason, I said to myself.

"I decided on civil disobedience and understood and knew the story of Jesus in the temple overthrowing the tables of the money changers and driving them out. . . . In 1969 I took responsibility for raids on draft boards in New York City. Subsequently, I was given permission by my order, the Society of Jesus, to undertake full-time peace work, that is, preaching, teaching and acting on my beliefs. The Community of Resistance grew, involving more and more people, including the young. And a new factor entered our lives, the informer.

"Informers have been with us all through history. Not, we assume, though in a democratic society or anyhow, not in American society, but they do exist and they are employed by the United States government. That Nazi nightmare of the informer amongst us is shared even by Americans. The use of friend against friend, and that is so, even though we know that informers, as a law enforcement tool, are unreliable and self-serving. And we also know bugged rooms and tapped phones, as we know from the Watergate affair. And in the name of what? What democratic principle?

"It began for me in a classroom in Rochester, and it culminates here in a courtroom in Camden. Three of those high school boys are dead; four are in VA hospitals for life; one in a mental ward; two were founders of Vietnam Veterans Against the War in Rochester. Many others I'm proud to say were conscientious objectors. And you should know that from May of 1970 to May of 1971 that there were a hundred and three thousand applications for conscientious objector status in this country."

Concluding his remarks, Father McGowan told the jury:

"Other Vietnams are in our future, not obvious and loud, but under cover and silent. For we are there already in Asia, Africa, and Latin America. Your decision then in our regard is not unreal. We do not ask for compassion, for something past, but ask courage from you to protest what is happening now.

"Go to Greenwich, New Jersey, and look upon the statue of three men, the tea destroyers, learn from them and free us all. Thank you, and I apologize for being so nervous."[3]

The jury deliberated for three days before announcing that the Camden 28, who had steadfastly admitted that they entered the draft board in Camden, fully intending to destroy draft records, were *not* guilty.

Teresa Grady smiles at these recollections, rays of afternoon sunshine sparkling through her grey-white hair. She speaks slowly, carefully, sorting through the years like precious seashells, laughing at the suggestion of heroism. No, Hollywood never approached her, not back in the 'sixties, not in the 'eighties when the nostalgia market flourished. And even if the dream-makers did make an offer she would probably send them, politely but firmly, away. There is no point, she would tell them, in romanticizing or sensational-izing her family's story. They are not an anti-war version of the "Partridge Family," or a Plowshare rendition of "Little House on the Prairie." The war in Vietnam finally ended, but there was no peace in the Grady home. There was separa-tion, hardship, loneliness. But when Teresa speaks of John, Sr., it is about his willingness to "pay up" for his beliefs, the contributions he made to peace, and the important and en-during things she, her children, and so many others have learned from him.

She knows that some people still disagree with and even hate her and John Grady for their stand on war; and she understands that while many people feel Vietnam was a tragic mistake, the wounds from that war have only recently begun to heal; much of the bitterness and many of the di-visions remain unresolved. To their friends and supporters, the Gradys are courageous, loving, dedicated to the cause of peace. To their critics, they have been and always will be little more than Pied Pipers of the peace movement's lunatic fringe. Teresa never doubted that John might go to prison, but this was really not the most important consideration. Thousands of people were going to prison for resisting the Vietnam War. Sometimes the rent was paid late, sometimes there wasn't a lot of food in the house. The FBI lingered and loitered, but the bureau's men resembled Keystone Cops rather than the slick, omnipotent, agents seen on television. They were too incompetent to really frighten anyone.

Sooner or later John and his fellow draft board invaders would be caught, that much was expected. In their group was the informer about whom Father McGowan would later testify, a man who urged them to turn in Gandhi for a gun, admit that in a violent nation like the U.S. nonviolence would never work. He provided them with the blueprints of the Camden draft board, tools, and even money. He would provide the FBI with their whereabouts.

John Grady and his friends had no illusions about stopping the war. One does not always act, John and Teresa would tell their children, in the hope of achieving some definable goal. Surely Sophie and Hans Scholl, and other young Germans who were executed for criticizing Adolph Hitler, knew that distributing anti-Nazi leaflets would not bring about the collapse of the Third Reich. Certainly members of the White Rose resistance movement had known many of their fellow Germans would call them ineffective, romantic adventurers, neurotics, even fools. Max Josef Metzger, a Catholic priest executed by the Gestapo in Brandenburg Prison, Berlin, on April 17, 1944, for refusing to cooperate with the German war effort had not kept Hitler from killing more Jews. Austrian peasant Franz Jägerstätten, beheaded by the German military as an "enemy of the state," did not bring about world peace when he declined—even after being offered the chance to avoid execution—to fight for the Third Reich. Even a million Danes wearing the yellow Star of David to prevent the Nazis from distinguishing between Jewish and non-Jewish citizens, even Danish workers who went on strike, refusing to repair German ships and nonviolently sabotaging the genocidal plans of the German command, could not stop the Holocaust. The point, said

John and Teresa, was not to look for some acceptable measure of success. The object was not to get elected to office, bring down a government, or be enshrined in history books, but merely to resist evil, to say, as Plowshare activists would declare at their trials two decades later, *"Not in my name."*

John Grady was finally cornered by forty agents with drawn guns. The informant had lied to the FBI, telling the bureau's agents that the Camden 28 were heavily armed with revolvers, rifles, and even grenades. John Grady held his hands high, and smiled. In his pockets were two pens, one hanky, and a set of car keys.

The Cold War may be ending, but Teresa Grady, who was recently arrested during a protest at Seneca Army Depot, does not believe the United States is prepared to relinquish the kind of myths and collective self-delusion that have inspired men to go to war for centuries. As the Berlin Wall comes down and pro-democracy movements sweep across Europe, she argues, our own leaders insist on congratulating themselves on the triumph of "peace through strength," then promptly set out to design, test, and deploy a whole new generation of atomic weapons. As the Soviet economy collapses, American politicians are more interested in praising the wonders of our "market economy" than in acknowledging that for millions of Americans life is a desperate day-to-day struggle to survive.

After fifty years of expanding our empire and building the mightiest army the world has ever known, there is little evidence that the United States is prepared to beat swords into plowshares. Teresa Grady isn't surprised that people believe we no longer need to worry about nuclear weapons. When the superpowers agree to stockpile only enough weapons to kill everyone in the world *ten or fifteen* rather than *thirty* times over, both governments tell their people this is tantamount to peace on earth.

"The Vietnam War ended but government subterfuge," says Teresa, "did not. The only difference between then and now is that we believe Big Brother when he tells us that WAR IS PEACE and LOVE IS HATE."

A gray, pock-marked sky, the wind filled with ice chips. Flurries of snow. The apartment had been so warm, sweet with incense, candles, and singing. A papier-mache Virgin Mary holding the baby Jesus in her arms, Joseph smiling, sheep and goats nuzzling into the manger, and the children forming a procession, singing hope and love and peace on earth. But here, on this bleak Manhattan street, the windows were barred, dimly lit. Inside there would be no creche or singing, no hot apple cider and freshly baked bread. The children sang, brushing snow from their eyebrows and noses. Christ, they announced, is alive and well, in you . . . in us . . . even in . . . there.

Clare Grady knew, because her father and mother had told her, that inside those walls were ordinary human beings, not demons or monsters. Women (there were no men inside) who needed love, affection, and understanding. Women who missed their own children terribly at this time of year, and who felt pain, loneliness, regret, guilt, sorrow, anger, hope, hopelessness. On this cold Christmas eve, she and her brother and sisters sang, loud and clear and with the passion they honestly felt.

Years later she would volunteer to work for the United Farm Workers and be sent to Los Angeles, a blue eyed, freckled, Irish-American young woman sitting behind a voter registration table in the burned-out streets of Watts. People in the neighborhood stopped to talk, offering ice cream, the men sometimes flirting. In the morning, promptly at 10:00 A.M., a middle-aged cowboy—ten-gallon hat, spurs, a cane with a cigarette holder perched upon its tip—would strut by, turn, pace back and forth, inhaling deeply and exhaling wobbly smoke rings. Waving the cane like a baton, he would laugh: "Baby," he'd say, "I'm gonna shoot right up to the stars . . . the moon . . . the sun . . . baby." Strutting and smoking, adjusting his hat or one of his spurs: "Baby . . . I'm gonna rise up . . . there . . . to the stars, moon, and sun, baby . . ."

California voters failed to pass Proposition 14, a law that would have ensured funding for labor elections for farmworkers, and Clare returned to New York's Lower East Side, drifting away from the church and even her family for a time. One day she heard something astonishing and frightening on the news. Two of her father's dearest friends, along with six others, had been arrested for entering a General Electric plant in King of Prussia, Pennsylvania. She watched and wondered, feeling confused and frightened by what she read.

At first she thought the demonstrators had been battering a nuclear-tipped weapon, and was relieved to discover the thing they had hammered was an unarmed nosecone. Reading the news accounts, she wondered what exactly the Plowshare Eight were trying to accomplish? Assuming they were trying to force the U.S. government to disarm, their action was little more than an exercise in futility, similar to asking government officials to hang or decapitate themselves. Certainly that would never happen. For some years, Clare had lived apart from the Catholic Left and, though she knew and respected those who'd taken part in the action at King of Prussia, the act of pounding on components for nuclear weapons seemed utterly pointless.

It would take some time for her to realize that Plowshare activists weren't really asking the government to *do* anything, even though the protesters hoped government officials would also take personal responsibility for disarmament. It was important, Clare would later realize, to have been outside of the movement, looking in from a critical, skeptical, and even rather judgmental viewpoint. She had grown up with the Catholic Left, watching the Berrigans, her own father, and friends engage in acts of resistance; nevertheless, it took her some time to grasp the real meaning or purpose in Plowshare actions. Later, during her own trial for engaging in a Plowshare action, she found it much easier to understand the jurors' decisions and the rude, often arrogant comments of the government prosecutor.

While she was still trying to sort out her feelings about Plowshare actions, Clare's brother John and sister Ellen went on trial for pounding on and pouring blood over a Trident atomic submarine. As the defendants stood in the hallway outside the courtroom, alternate jurors approached them, apologizing and explaining that in fact they really did believe much of what John and Ellen were saying, but were constrained by the judge from interpreting the law in the defendants' favor. When the proceedings ended and several state police officers led John and Ellen away in handcuffs, one of the jurors told Clare that "it felt like we were crucifying Christ."

On Thanksgiving Day 1983, Clare Grady and six others— Elizabeth McAlister, Dean Hammer, Jackie Allen, Kathleen Rumpf, Vern Rossman, and Karl Smith—entered Griffiss Air

Force Base in Rome, New York. They walked into the hangar where B-52s, wings sagging and noses pressed to the metal walls, were waiting to be retrofitted with cruise missiles, small first-strike weapons designed to fly by sensors on automatic pilot, following the contours of a landscape, dipping and rising, staying low to avoid radar, each one smashing into its target with the force of fifteen Hiroshima bombs. Each B-52 would carry approximately twenty Cruise missiles, or the equivalent of 300 Hiroshimas.

Clare and the others poured bottles of their own blood on the hangar floor and over the planes, pounded with hammers on the bomb-bay doors, and pasted photos of children on the sides of the planes. Their hammering sounded sharp and loud in the early morning stillness, but no one appeared. They regrouped on the tarmac, praying and giving thanks for a successful action. After singing and dancing for about an hour, they walked out to the road and unfurled a banner. Many cars passed by and finally a security guard approached. "I don't care if it is Thanksgiving," he told the protesters. "You people just can't stay here." "Well," they replied, "you might want to check out Hangar 101 first. We just did a disarmament action there."

Soon they were kneeling in the mud, hands cuffed behind their backs, wrists lashed tightly together with thin strips of black plastic, M-16s pointing at their heads. They were placed on a bus and ordered not to talk. Two, three, eight hours passed. Their hands swelled, wrists and bladders ached, and they were given no food or drink, allowed no trips to the bathroom. For breaking the silence, Kathleen Rumpf was taken off the bus and deposited, hands cuffed behind her back, in a puddle of water.

Inside the Syracuse Public Safety Building, Clare Grady

stood naked on a platform, a matron ordering her to soap, "No, more there. There. Scrub." Clare had never been in jail. "Squat," the matron ordered, "and cough." "Move." "Sit." "Put these on." A set of baggy prison clothes, a harried call to her family, the phone going dead in her hand. A rule book thrust forward: "Know this by heart before you reach the cellblock." A newscaster: "The maximum sentence for the Griffiss action could be twenty-five years."

She tried to talk to her sister through the thick glass separating prisoners and visitors. Just an elbow away, Elizabeth McAlister was asking her husband, Philip Berrigan, to give their three children her love. Clare thought about Liz, how she might go to prison for twenty-five years. During the first few humiliating hours in jail Clare really hadn't cried, but now she began to weep, great shoulder-shaking sobs.

At the Griffiss Plowshare trial, Daniel Ellsberg testified— though he was not allowed to do so in front of the jury— that competition for nuclear superiority had transformed the United States into a *National Security State*. The consequences of this are a government that makes many decisions in secret, without consulting the people, and a people that distrusts government officials. This secrecy, Ellsberg explained, reduces the control which Congress, the American people, and the courts have over democratic process. Ellsberg testified that even U.S. Presidents are occasionally unaware of important policy decisions. For example, John F. Kennedy did not know that Dwight D. Eisenhower had delegated authority for a nuclear attack to field commanders. When he first took office, Kennedy heard rumors that field commanders had the power to initiate a nuclear attack in Europe or the Pacific. Ellsberg was hired to find out whether such secret order was in place, and eventually learned the rumor was based in fact. Kennedy kept this policy and, unknown to the American people, so did Lyndon Johnson. When asked whether the policy was in place, both Kennedy and Johnson denied they were continuing Eisenhower's decision.

Richard Falk has written:

> Ever since Hiroshima, a whole set of antidemocratic political arrangements have emerged and become permanent features of the governing process in the name of national security. The early insistence on secrecy culminated in sending Julius and Ethel Rosenberg to the electric chair in the first instance of capital punishment for espionage in the history of the United States. Protecting atomic secrets made eminent sense when the consequences could, in the public mind, lead directly and ultimately to a Soviet-engineered nuclear Pearl Harbor. From this premise has evolved the buildup of a huge intelligence and secret police establishment, the insistence on a classification system so rigid that on occasions an author has lost access to his own work because of clearance difficulties, and a permanent 'enemies list' that has been used to justify surveillance and domestic spying as routine exercises of governmental authority has evolved.[4]

Elizabeth McAlister described how, after watching *The Day After* with Philip Berrigan and their three children, she told them that soon she would be taking direct action to resist the arms race, to say no to the "idolatry of nuclear weapons." "I have three choices," McAlister told the jury and Judge Munson: "Go to a safe place—that is no option. Pretend the threat is not there. Do not read, do not think. But we become part of the problem. Or ask, 'How can I best love my children, give them some hope for the future, do something to make that future a reality.'" "We now see," McAlister continued, "that the bomb controls national life, attitudes, psychologies, the economy, international relations." McAlister told the court about Dorothy Day's belief that "the bomb is not just 'out there.' It is also within us. Before we detonated it, we fashioned it . . . it arose out of the depth of our own souls. It came from us and is now enthroned . . ."[5]

Clare Grady recalled watching television when she was a child and seeing Vietnamese children who'd been scorched with napalm. She told the judge about her father's arrest for destroying draft files, how she and her family had attended the trial, and how the jury had refused to convict the Camden 28, acting instead on its own collective conscience. In the tenth grade she'd seen the film *Hiroshima and Nagasaki,* and had never been able to forget the sight of terribly burned human beings. In the hangar at Griffiss Air Force Base, said Clare, she had seen the "hugeness" of a B-52 and understood the destructive power of these planes. She and the others had pasted photos of friends and family to the fuselage of one plane, stained it with their own blood, and struck it repeatedly with hammers, thus "symbolically" disarming this weapon of mass destruction. Our action, Clare declared, was an act of conscience. We acted out of a sense of responsibility.

We cannot worship God *and* nuclear weapons, the Griffiss Plowshare defendants told the judge and jury. To be forced to do so would be a violation of the First Amendment to the U.S. Constitution, which states that "Congress shall make no law respecting an establishment of religion, or prohibiting the free exercise thereof . . ." The defendants told the court that they were Judeo-Christians (Biblical people), seeking in their lives to be faithful to God. The government, Clare and the others argued, was trying to force them into a "false worship" of nuclear weapons, and the only way they could be true to their own faith, and the guarantees the Constitution gave them, was to violate laws protecting these atomic idols.

*"You shall not make carved images for yourself . . . you shall not bow down to worship them"* (Deut. 5:8-9, NEB). *"You shall not make yourself gods of cast metal"* (Exod. 34:17, NEB). *"They shall beat their swords into plowshares and their spears into pruning hooks; nation shall not lift sword against nation nor ever again be trained for war"* (Mic. 4:3).

In a brief offered to the court, participants in the Griffiss Plowshares action carefully articulated their belief that citizens were being asked, indeed forced, to accept idolatry, to worship nuclear weapons.

While the Constitution claims that "Congress shall make no law respecting an establishment of religion, or prohibiting the free exercise thereof . . ." (Amendment I), a religion has been established in and by this country that violates the conscience of its citizens, *the cult of national sovereignty is the major religion.* This cult, as we will show, has all the dimensions of a religion, and worship of the imperial god is required of all. The nation-state/empire has become our god. For when one analyzes the implications of sovereignty (as in national sovereignty), it means divinity and nothing less.

We do not quarrel with patriotism, with love for one's own country. We do not quarrel with the need to respect—and require respect for—one's real needs as a country. Our difficulties are rooted in the reality that, in these days, we are citizens of a country with imperial claims, policies, and weapons. And the more imperial a nation seeks to become, the more it threatens religious freedom, because in its lust to be number one, it does not stop at usurping the authority even of God.

It may be truthfully argued that the United States does not make overt claims that our nation or its leaders are gods. (Such would be too unsophisticated.) Still, our country and its leadership (as well as other "imperialist" countries and their leaderships—the Soviet Union, China, etc.) sees itself as the "engine of history." McGeorge Bundy called the United States "the locomotive at the head of mankind [sic] pulling the caboose of humanity along behind." Any engine-of-history outlook requires the displacement of the *one* who is the *Lord of History.*

We assert that the nation-state as "god" has created idols that all its citizens, in the name of loyalty and patriotism, are required to *worship* and *to trust in.* This is a violation of our freedom of religion and *worship.*[6]

Assistant U.S. Attorney Joseph A. Pavone demanded to know more about the Griffiss action: Who helped plan it? Who drove the defendants to the site? Who attended their meetings and where had they been held? "I will not say who else was there. I will say who took responsibility for going onto Griffiss," Clare replied. "I will not speak for anyone else." Pavone warned Clare she could be held in contempt of court, then paced the courtroom, waiting for a reply. Clare Grady sat in silence. U.S. Attorney Frederick Scullin declined to charge the defendant with contempt, and the trial continued.

The judge did not accept the Griffiss Plowshare defendants' arguments, and remained unpersuaded by the testimony of expert witnesses, instead sentencing some defendants to two, others to three years in prison. Altogether, Clare spent fifteen months in Alderson Federal Penitentiary. Now, seven years later, Clare Grady sits in a rocking chair, nursing her year-old baby and pondering what, quite obviously, is a difficult, even painful, question.

"Would I go to prison again, now that I have a child? Well, no, not while I'm nursing her. I'm aware, of course, that so many women around the world do not have a choice in the matter. Women in El Salvador and Guatemala for example, are raped, killed, disappear . . . even while they're nursing their babies. It makes no difference to the U.S. Congress whose members are funding the killers, or the people who are actually doing the killing, whether the victim is a nursing mother.

"I remember lying on the bed one night shortly after Leah was born, with this tiny person on my chest, this life so absolutely dependent on me. And thinking: 'What if I was living in a warzone, pursued by death squads and military units? Or what if I was a refugee on the border of Honduras, or in one of the concentration camps we've established in Texas for Central American refugees fleeing from death and destruction? What would I do? Could I take it?' And I just couldn't imagine it.

"No . . . I don't like to think about the actual planning of a Plowshare action . . . I can't foresee it in real concrete terms right now . . . but I also know that sometimes things happen, mysteriously, in ways you would never imagine . . . Oh dear," she pauses and closes her eyes, "this is a very hard question. Very hard. I've known many women, both friends before I went to prison and friends in prison, who have lived separated from their children. And while I don't make light of their pain, I know that it doesn't have to be a totally negative thing. In prison we actually formed, or you might say continued, our community. We supported one another. We talked, worked together, and got to know so many wonderful people who were in prison only because they were poor or people of color, or both. I know that Liz missed her children terribly, but she also knew they were being cared for in community, loved and nurtured by people in community. I don't think it's ever easy to go to prison and leave your children, but if we are living in community at least the separation won't be quite so abrupt."

"It's very hard to answer," adds Ellen Grady, imprisoned for hammering on and pouring blood over a Trident submarine, and kept in solitary confinement for her refusal to submit to repeated vaginal searches. "Because in our lives, our mother was always there for us. So that's what I was always taught: To be a mother is to be there for your children. And so, thinking about getting arrested and being away from my children for a long, long time is a very, very hard thing to do. I haven't thought about it in any concrete terms, and I haven't been in that situation yet. But in terms of my marriage to Peter, it's something we've talked about, something we're committed to in our marriage. Peter was just in jail for thirty days for refusing to pay a hundred-dollar fine imposed after he was arrested at Seneca Army Depot, and, while that time was very hard, it was also very good because I realize that the community of people I live with are supportive. I found out that people will help with the children. I can ask for help, and it's possible to do this kind of resistance work if you have a community of people to help you."

"I would just like to add," says Clare, "that when Leah stops nursing, and if I felt called to do another Plowshare action, then it would be an entirely new thing, a new exploration. I'd just have to take it one step at a time. You really can't sit around and plan a Plowshare action like you would a vacation, or new job. Liz McAlister once said that each time you do one of these things, like a Plowshare action, you have to go through a fire, a kind of crucible. No matter how many times you do it, it's always new."

"Having children," adds John Grady, Jr., who was sent to prison for the same Plowshare action in which Ellen, and her husband Peter DeMott, took part, "definitely changes the way you think about things, for a lot of practical purposes. But when I look at Plowshares, and the issues the movement raises both for those who participate and the community at large, I feel that I would be doing more for the children by taking part in an action. Laurie and I really haven't talked about it that much, so the consequences to our family, right now, are just unknown. But it's really a lifeline to see our friends in court these past few months. To know someone's there, someone's really keeping hope alive."

"Why do we do the kinds of things that other Irish Catholic families might find bizarre or even crazy?" asks Maryanne Grady, who lives with her husband, Oscar, and their four children in a two-bedroom apartment in Queens. "Well, I think it's because we've been given a certain knowledge about what the Pentagon is doing. How the military squanders our money. And what will really happen if we ever use nuclear weapons . . . even one or two . . . anywhere in the world. And because we, as Catholics, as a family, and as Americans, keep asking why there are thirty-seven million people who don't have health insurance in this, the richest country on earth; why there are two million people living in the streets; why there are millions unemployed, on drugs, in prison.

"You see, our parents taught not from books, but by example. By their actions, as well as family discussions and reading. And they stressed faith. Our faith in God to do the right thing; the understanding of how the poor are treated, and what we need to do if we wish to create justice in the world. So if you're given this knowledge, then it's important that you do something with it. Take a stand. Make a contribution.

"When we were younger, my father and friends put their lives on the line for what they believed in. They risked losing everything—jobs, friends, even family. And that's what so much of the rest of the world is doing right now. Every day, on a day-to-day basis in places like Guatemala, El Salvador, South Africa. That's what Archbishop Oscar Romero found out—that you cannot serve the rich *and the poor.* That's what so many of the brave nuns and priests in Central American have discovered, and why they've been martyred, tortured, and killed. You just have to make some painful and sometimes even life-threatening choices."

In the log home where John Grady DeFlaun lives in community with his wife Laurie, Peter DeMott, and his wife Ellen Grady, the babies are dressed for christening. Children gambol through the yard, and there's an air of cheerful chaos. DeMott, former seminarian, Marine veteran of the Vietnam War, imprisoned several times for Plowshare actions, shakes hands and exchanges greetings with friends and relatives. Ellen Grady hugs each new arrival. John Grady DeFlaun watches his small son race, waddle, and stumble across the yard. John's sister, Teresa, holds her infant son's head while the priest anoints his forehead. The babies are blessed, the bread and wine passed, hugs and greetings of "Peace Be With You" exchanged. No one talks about prison, yet everyone knows that next year or the year after there may be fewer here to celebrate. Like people everywhere, the Gradys would like to believe that ending the Cold War really means the world's nations, particularly the superpowers, will soon commence beating swords into plowshares. They would very much like to think that the usurpation of democracy that Daniel Ellsberg and others say has accompanied the arms race will end, that our own secret police apparatus (Federal Bureau of Investigation, Central Intelligence Agency, National Security Agency) will soon be disbanded, that America's political prisoners (Jean Gump, Father Carl Kabat, Helen Woodson, and many others) will be freed and the national security state become a thing of the past. But they see no evidence of this happening, now or in the near future.

Indeed, Philip Berrigan sums up the feeling of the Gradys and the Plowshare movement when he writes:

> The current START talks (sham or scam or both?) "should shake complacency from us. They follow exactly their 6,000 predecessors, with a priority on public relations. (From such expense and verbiage, not one nuclear warhead has been destroyed). The Superpowers trade off their older missiles like the American Minuteman II for new families of First Strike weapons—Cruise missiles, 'gravity' (penetrating) bombs,

Trident 11, the B-2. START requires no halt in nuclear testing, no curbs on producing new warheads nor recycling old ones. Moreover, it counts a strategic bomber like the B-1 or B-2 as a single weapon, even though it carries up to 22 hydrogen bombs."[7]

The Gradys recall their father and mother talking about the "long haul" of resistance. Not just a few years, or even a decade, but a lifetime of prayers and protests. Sometimes it's been necessary to go to prison. Undoubtedly, they say, it will be necessary to do so again.

# Notes

1. Thomas Merton, *The Nonviolent Alternative* (New York: Farrar Straus Giroux, 1971), 148.

2. Theodore Bikel, *Folksongs and Footnotes* (Cleveland: The World Publishing Company, 1960) 180–1.

3. United States District Court, District of New Jersey. *United States of America* v. *Terry E. Buckalew, et als.*, Defendants. Transcript of Proceedings. Testimony of Father Edward J. McGowan, S.J., 1863–66.

4. Robert Jay Lifton and Richard Falk, *INDEFENSIBLE WEAPONS: The Political and Psychological Case Against Nuclearism* (New York: Basic Books, 1982), 139.

5. Testimony of Elizabeth McAlister, quoted in *GRIFFISS PLOWSHARES ACTION AND TRIAL: Trial Sequence, Notes and Texts of Testimonies, Comment and News Coverage* (Syracuse: Sarah Appleton Weber, 1984), 92.

6. Arthur J. Laffin and Anne Montgomery, eds., *Swords Into Plowshares: Nonviolent Direct Action For Disarmament* (New York: Harper & Row, 1987), 178–9.

7. Philip Berrigan, "Swedish & English Plowshares," *The New Year One*, Vol. XVII No. 2, Jonah House, Baltimore, May 1990, 8.

# Seven

## *Politics and Passion Plays: The Future of Plowshare Actions*

> ... I had a letter from a distinguished senator
> before I left, because he had read about
> possible defense cuts, a reduction in the
> defense budget, saying take that money and
> spend it for a cause that he felt was very
> worthy. And I had to write him back and say,
> "Look, that isn't the way it's going to work."
> That isn't the way it's going to work.
>
> PRESIDENT GEORGE BUSH

At the Atlantic Life Community retreat, a semi-annual gathering of Plowshare activists and their supporters, and possibly one or two curious FBI agents, some of the children are playing soccer. Others are painting a free-flowing collage of peace signs, flowers, and atomic weapons, their collective imagination blooming across a huge sheet of paper. Philip Berrigan is once again in jail, and several people who usually attend these retreats are missing.

Adults who aren't helping take care of the children squeeze into a meeting room, waiting for Elizabeth McAlister to begin her presentation. She leans forward in her chair, scanning her notes, smiling and waving to friends, or perhaps it would be more accurate to say members of her extended family. Some of those attending the retreat are new—writers and scholars drawn to the retreat by curiosity about the Berrigans and the Plowshare movement, young Catholic workers who've spent a year or two living among and working with the homeless, college students heading home after a summer of ladling out soup in the hot, drug-infested, crime-ridden inner city. But most of the people gathered here are veterans of the movement that began in the Baltimore Customs House, at the Catonsville and Camden draft boards, in front of military induction centers; the resistance that grew into teach-ins and sit-ins, moratoriums and strikes, mass demonstrations and countless acts of civil disobedience. They are more than old friends, their bonds tightly woven by a quarter-century spent, separately and in groups, going in and out of federal courtrooms, in and out of jails and prisons, living out an agenda that many of their fellow Americans find peculiar, ineffective, even crazy.

Now the room is almost quiet. Warm. Comfortable. Muffled cries from the children's soccer game. Gil Ott, Vietnam combat veteran and member of Veterans For Peace, an international organization of military veterans dedicated to abolishing war, sits on the floor, legs stretched out and back to the wall. Ellen Grady nurses her baby in one corner, Tom Lewis opens his sketch pad, Dean Hammer seems to be meditating. Elizabeth McAlister sits cross-legged in her chair and, glancing about the room one more time, begins to speak from her notes.

"Peace is breaking out all over," she says. "British Prime Minister Margaret Thatcher and the *New York Times* pronounce the Cold War over. The Soviets withdraw from Afghanistan. The United States and the Soviet Union negotiate to cut nuclear weapons and conventional forces in Europe.

"President Bush proclaims that fresh breezes are blowing, *and* even acknowledges that—in the world's richest nation— there are people sleeping on the streets who would rather not be there."

A nice scenario, says McAlister, fed to a public, indeed a world population, willing, out of a desperate longing for peace, to accept such totally false conclusions. Yet even as the Cold War is pronounced over, the United States continues its quest for nuclear superiority. Even as the champagne glasses tinkle and the toasts are made at Soviet-American dinners, the Air Force continues testing its long range MX missiles and heralds its new Stealth bomber. Even as the president talks about a "thousand points of light," the Navy commissions yet another, and another, Trident submarine, underwater doomsday machines that lurk in the world's seas, waiting for the command to end all life on earth. And even as political and military magicians paint the facade of peace, stroke by master stroke, newspaper and magazine articles describe decades of duplicity and deceit at nuclear power plants:

- The release of plutonium, one of the most lethal substances known to science, into the drinking water of communities near Rocky Flats, Colorado, where triggers for atomic warheads are made
- Fires, equipment failures, irradiated water at the Sa-

vannah River plutonium-processing facilities in South Carolina

- High rates of cancer and other health problems among residents living near nuclear power plants, weapons factories, and atomic test sites
- Government and corporate incompetence, cover-ups, and lying to keep the public from understanding the real dangers of radiation exposure

And the cost to begin cleaning up forty-five years of environmental poisoning is enormous: a minimum of 100 billion dollars to encase sections of buildings in concrete, then bury them for a thousand years . . . scoop oceans of contaminated soil into lead-lined storage bins . . . test streams, lakes and aquifers for traces of radioactive isotopes and plutonium . . . filter poisoned water . . . fight lawsuits on behalf of sick and dying people who live near sites where bombs or missile components are made. To save ourselves from our enemies, it appears we've been willing to poison our children, and their children's children.

"Times like these," McAlister continues, "test the meaning of hope. The temptation is to separate hope and history. Hope in God's plan for the universe, hope in the triumph of justice and peace, is inseparable from faith, but as people generally use the word, hope describes feelings and sentiments. And feelings and sentiments can immobilize hope— can detach it from the realities of history, can enable us to avoid our individual responsibility to be part of the process, to create hope.

"Yet cynicism about the changes taking place around us is as immobilizing as misplaced hope. In politics nothing produces burnout faster than the idea that the more things change, the more they remain the same. If victories are only illusions, why struggle? No one who struggles for justice can expect 'success!' It is not even clear what success is in any given case.

"The Cold War is diminishing," says McAlister, "but the arms race continues." The Cold War may be ending, but the "institutions that have provided the energy for it are *still* intact." According to Seymour Melman, professor emeritus of industrial engineering at Columbia University:

> Military spending is 6 percent of G.N.P., but it pays for the services of 25 to 30 percent of all our nation's engineers and scientists and accounts for 70 percent of all Federal research and development money, $41 billion in 1988. . . . The central administrative office of the Department of Defense has a staff of 120,000 and controls more than 35,000 prime contracting companies. Such managerial organizations do not readily relinquish decision-making power. And many members of Congress have become accustomed to functioning as virtual marketing managers for military companies, bases and laboratories in their districts.[1]

The Cold War may end, but preparations for war do not. Indeed, the Pentagon's buzzword for the 'nineties, "low-intensity conflict," translates to installing "friendly" governments in Central America, then arming, training, and, if need be, fighting beside these client armies. Meanwhile, in the U.S. and Soviet Union, men and women continue to sit in underground bunkers, watching Pac-man screens, sipping coffee, and waiting for a coded call that could well mean an atomic attack. In think tanks and scientific laboratories, men and women still work feverishly to design and build a sci-fi shield around our nation's borders. During space missions, astronauts launch spy satellites so we can continue to spy on our newfound friends.

The national treasury, plundered by the military for decades, continues to support torturers and assassins in various parts of the world, while in our own country the legions of homeless grow, drugs decimate the nation's youth, bridges collapse, acid rain destroys forests and lakes, schools close for lack of funding, racism poisons the melting pot, and crime holds millions of "free" citizens hostage. Dr. Melman writes:

> From 1947 to 1987, according to the Federal Government's own estimates, the United States spent $7.6 trillion on the military, a sum roughly equal to the total value of the nation's plant and equipment, plus the value of its civilian infrastructure. This means that since 1947, our military has used up resources sufficient to rebuild nearly everything that is manmade in the United States.[2]

"For the first time," McAlister concludes, "we are determining the destinies of the earth in a comprehensive and irreversible manner. The immediate danger may be either nuclear war or the industrial plundering of ozone and rain forests and breast milk and background radiation and water contamination. The heart of the creation, the human, is going through a profound crisis. We grasp the moment or we die."

On Monday morning, puffy-eyed but cheerful after two days and three nights of workshops and discussions, people gather in the dining room again, chatting quietly over breakfast. At approximately 9:00 A.M., the phone rings and Dean Hammer, jailed for his part in the Plowshare Eight action and again for his involvement with the Griffiss Plowshare group, is called into the kitchen where he listens carefully, smiling and nodding from time to time. Returning to the dining room, he announces that early that morning seven Plowshare activists, some swimming through the garbage-strewn waters of the Thames River, others paddling canoes, entered the Naval Underwater Systems Center in New London, Connecticut. Paddling on their backs to the USS *Pennsylvania Trident* submarine, then treading water, Jackie Allen and Kathy Boylan scratched DEATH on the side of the ship. Like breaching whales they leaped again and again from the water, pounding with their hammers on the Trident's slick black side. Washed downriver by the tide, Homer White climbed to shore and, dressed in a wetsuit and waddling in his flippers, tried to enter the submarine base. Elmer Maas and Art Laffin canoed to the Trident's tail, hammering and pouring blood, before boarding the ship and continuing to hammer. As sailors sprayed them with a hose, Maas and Laffin kneeled on the Trident's stern and prayed.

The protesters were removed from the submarine, but managed to leave a videotape showing Hiroshima shortly after the Enola Gay had dropped *Little Boy* on that city. They also left a Salvadoran cross and booklets describing how the superpowers are turning the high seas into nuclear free-fire zones. Later, Jackie Allen will undoubtedly tell the judge about her work with Connecticut's homeless, explaining how money that should be spent to feed the poor is used instead to construct an atomic armada, each ship carrying the equivalent of 6,400 Hiroshimas, the total fleet, 128,000 Hiroshimas. Sister Anne Montgomery, member of the Plowshare Eight and jailed repeatedly for her opposition to war, may talk about seeing, in the frozen eyes of the dead on Manhattan's streets, the true mirror of military spending. Jim Reale will say that he is unwilling to live in a world which spends one million dollars a minute on preparations for war, while fifty thousand people die each day from starvation.

According to Jim Sasser, chairman of the Senate Budget Committee, the so-called peace dividend is a "rubber check": "To put all of that as simply as possible," says Sasser, "the Pentagon gets $287 billion in the budget just passed for fiscal 1990. Under the exercise in 'austerity' proposed by the Secretary, the Pentagon would get more than $290 billion annually through the mid-90s." Defense Secretary Dick Cheney's budget proposal "assumes continuation of virtually all of the Pentagon's priorities and programs, and it eschews entirely a fundamental reevaluation of our military establishment in light of our changing security needs. Such a reappraisal has to be the beginning point."[3]

The defendants will speak *pro se,* without an attorney, and there will be no courtroom histrionics, no evangelical strutting and fretting or trumpeting of legal brilliance. The defendants will speak quietly, trying to explain what brought them to the Naval Underwater Systems Center; telling judge and jury that, like people everywhere, they too want desperately to believe that the arms race is over, a new vision of international cooperation about to replace decades of vitriolic rhetoric; they too want to believe that perestroika is sweeping our own nation; that one day soon the American people will live in a bona fide constitutional, multi-party democracy. That one day the handful of wealthy individuals who comprise the National Security Council will relinquish their oligarchical grip on foreign policy; that some day the CIA will be a training school for nonviolent conflict resolution, rather than violent coups d'etat and political assassination; that perhaps the Pentagon will be a think tank for environmental survival, instead of the command center for global destruction.

"But no change will happen," they will declare, quoting Elizabeth McAlister, "without the participation of masses of people. By themselves, elites cannot and will not steer complex societies along new paths. Democracy has become the precondition for economic development and peace."

In the boardrooms of General Dynamics and other defense contractors, say Plowshare activists, computer charts will be scrutinized, profit margins debated, losses and gains projected. But there will be no panic. President Bush has decided not to deploy a new, more powerful version of the Lance missile in Europe, but there are still 1,400 free-fall bombs, carried by the F-111 and other Europe-based aircraft, 200 anti-submarine depth bombs, 700 aging Lance missiles, and 1,200 nuclear artillery shells. (The W-79 artillery shells stored in Europe and the Seneca Army Depot in upstate New York were recently found to be defective. According to the Defense Department, a sudden impact could cause these shells to detonate, scattering plutonium, one of the deadliest carcinogens known to science, about a large area.) B-52, B-1B, and FB-111 bombers continue to carry the Short-Range Attack Missile—A, or SCRAM-As, and will soon carry the new model, SCRAM-2, which is under development for deployment in 1993. The SCRAM-A is an air-to-surface missile that carries the W-69 nuclear warhead with an estimated explosive yield of 170,000 tons of TNT, or

11 to 13 times the explosive power of the bomb that de-stroyed Hiroshima. On June 8, 1990, Secretary of Defense Dick Cheney ordered the Air Force to temporarily remove these attack missiles from bombers, following warnings by the directors of three U.S. nuclear weapons laboratories that they could leak plutonium in an accident. And there is more to come—a new air-to-surface nuclear missile that can be carried on the F-16 fighters based in Europe; the F-15E nu-clear strike aircraft now being built. And the Air Force is de-veloping an air-to-surface missile, the short-range Attack Missile-Tactical, with a range of 250 miles.

Orders may be slow for a while, the Berrigans and friends argue, but they are hardly about to stop. Empires, say Plow-share activists, may change, shrink, or expand, but do not collapse overnight. Some swords may be beaten into plow-shares, but others have been designed, are being tested, and will soon replace them.

The Cold War may be over, but the arms race is clearly not. Peace, say Plowshare activists, does not come through strength, but through love. It would be wonderful to believe that events in Eastern Europe will convince the superpowers to disarm, but that would mean a radical transformation of our own wartime economy, something those who profit from designing and manufacturing weapons of mass de-struction will strongly resist. It would mean an open, not secret, government, a constitutional democracy rather than a national security state; a democratic restructuring that, Plowshare activists argue, the CIA, the National Security Council, and multinational corporations whose shareholders make enormous profits from the arms race will just never accept. Moreover, the arms race has spread far beyond the boundaries of the superpowers. In the mad scramble to secure the secret of annihilation, nine countries have acquired the technology and materials needed to build atomic weapons. Five of these—the United States, the Soviet Union, China, France, and Britain—are bona fide members of the nuclear club, while four others—Israel, India, Pakistan, and South Africa—are suspected to be working members. Soon Iraq may also have atomic weapons, then Libya and Iran. For forty-five years, argue the Berrigans and friends, the superpowers have set a mad, diabolical pace, building generation after generation of more precise, more deadly atomic weapons. The leadership of both nations has insisted that these massive stockpiles are a symbol of strength and national security, the only real way to maintain world peace. Perhaps once their stockpiles reached the point of absurd overkill, Soviet and American leaders no longer believed their own convoluted rhetoric; perhaps, they do not believe it now. But both nations have first-strike weapons in place, while the leaders of other nations rush to demonstrate their own country's technological genius. In an unstable world where blood feuds, vendettas, and sheer hatred often overwhelm reason, it is quite possible that sooner or later someone will push the Armageddon button.

There is nothing they would rather do, say Plowshare activists, than join hands with the Joint Chiefs of Staff from the United States and Soviet Union, singing and dancing to welcome the dawning of a new world, one where the word of the Gospels would replace the mad rhetoric of the arms race. How wonderful it would be to embrace President Bush, the director of the FBI, CIA operatives, and judges who have sentenced men and women to prison for their opposition to war. To join those who design, build, deploy, and profit from nuclear weapons in beating the world's atomic arsenals into plowshares. Plowshare activists say they do not wish to be doomsayers or prophets of the apocalypse. Moreover, they acknowledge that for the first time since 1945, there is genuine hope for peace. People are reaching out to former adversaries, hugging and often weeping at the discovery that they can love instead of hate one another. There is a new and powerful urge among people everywhere, say the Berrigans and friends, to save the planet from ecological destruction, a desire to transcend old animosities, break down old fears and arbitrary borders, and work together to stop the elephant from becoming extinct, the rain forests from turning into deserts, and the oceans from becoming oil slicks and toxic cesspools. We stand, say the Berrigans, *et al.*, on an exciting and dangerous precipice, peering into our own demise yet inspired by new possibilities, by hope, and by the vision of living together as one people.

But in spite of all these new developments, there will be more Plowshare actions, more trials, more men and women sentenced to prison terms for their belief: "The heart of the creation, the human, is going through a profound spiritual crisis. We grasp the moment, or we die." The Cold War may be over, say Plowshare activists, but our fascination with war remains strong, our willingness to destroy the planet, through building and deploying nuclear weapons, unchecked. The Berlin Wall may have come down, Germany may be reunited, and doctrinaire communism may be defunct in Eastern Europe, but the aide standing next to President Gorbachev, and the military attache next to President Bush each carry a "black box" strapped to their wrist. Inside of each box is the code for universal suicide. No one knows when, or under what circumstances, the code might be activated. Americans and people everywhere, say Plowshare activists, must be willing to give up their false sense of security, leave their possessions behind, and relinquish the illusion of freedom, to see that this never happens. The struggle is lifelong, a commitment to peace and social justice that has nothing to do with political victories or measurable success. When he was sentenced to ten years in prison for speaking out against militarism, Eugene V. Debs told the court:

> Your Honor, years ago I recognized my kinship with all living beings, and I made up my mind that I was not one bit better than the meanest on earth. I said then, I say now, that while there is a lower class I am in it; while there is a criminal element, I am of it; while there is a soul in prison, I am not free. . . . Your Honor, I have stated in this court that I am opposed to the form of our present government; that I am opposed to the social system in which we live; that I believe in the change of both—but by perfectly peaceable and orderly means. . . . Let the people take heart and hope everywhere, for the cross is bending, the midnight is passing, and joy cometh with the morning.[4]

Seventy years later, the Berrigans and friends are acting out their own belief that the cross is bending, the midnight passing. To see them at Atlantic Life Community retreats, to visit them in prison or read their writings, one cannot help being impressed by their commitment and inspired by their *joie de vivre.* As long as the weapons remain in place, say the Berrigans and friends, as long as our nation's streets are filled with homeless, our prisons crowded with the poor, our children dying from overdoses of drugs and despair, and our government continuing to ignore the collapse of our cities,

Plowshare actions will continue. Men and women like Molly Rush, Carl and Paul Kabat, Helen Woodson, Elmer Maas, Martin Holladay, Anne Montgomery, Jean Gump and Joe Gump, Elizabeth McAlister, Kathleen Rumpf, Ellen Grady, and many others will go to prison for their beliefs.

# Notes

1. Seymour Melman, "The Peace Dividend, What to Do With the Cold War Money," *The New York Times,* Sunday, December 17, 1989, F3.

2. Ibid.

3. Jim Sasser, "The 'Peace Dividend': A Rubber Check." *The New York Times,* Tuesday, December 19, 1989, A27.

4. Sidney Lens, *Radicalism in America* (New York: Thomas & Crowel Company, 1966), 256.

# *Epilogue*

The atmosphere inside Philadelphia's University Lutheran Church was part revival meeting, part wake. Philip and Daniel Berrigan sat in the back row, eyes closed, heads bowed, apparently deep in thought. Between them Frida Berrigan, looking anxious and a little afraid, listened to friends praise the Plowshare Eight's efforts to beat swords into plowshares. After more than a decade of appealing the three-to-ten-year prison sentences they received for taking part in the first Plowshares action, the Eight were about to be resentenced. Philip, now in his sixties, and Dan, nearly seventy, might well spend the rest of their lives in a federal penitentiary.

A final prayer, and the procession began to General Electric's Aerospace division at 32nd and Chestnut. Outside the church, a young girl handed out small white candles in paper cups, but the wind made it difficult to keep them lit. A full moon, fuzzy around the edges and very pale, balanced on the city's skyline. The procession moved down Chestnut Street. Philip, Dan, John Schuchardt, and Molly Rush stood at the entrance to GE, holding a banner that read:

GENERAL ELECTRIC. THE CRIME IS HERE.

GE security guards dodged in and out of the building, snapping Polaroid photographs of the Berrigans and their supporters. Gusts of wind caught the Plowshare Eight's banner, making it flap like a disembodied wing.

"We come here," said the Berrigans and friends, "because this corporation, like so many others, continues to work on weapons of mass destruction. Ten years ago this was true. Today this is true. The witness begun at King of Prussia must continue wherever these diabolical weapons are designed, tested, manufactured, or deployed."

A Catholic priest related a story about a Russian immigrant who lived to be 101 years old. Shortly before his death the old man told his parish priest about seeing, on the evening news, a tank pulling a plow through a Soviet wheat field. "Imagine, a tank pulling a plow instead of a gun," the immigrant had said. "Think of it. That's what tanks are for. That's what they should be used for. Feeding, not killing human beings." The centennarian had waited all his life to see such a thing, never quite believing he would actually watch a Soviet tank be transformed into a plowshare.

To passersby, the rally at General Electric must have seemed a curious, even an anachronistic event. Wasn't the Cold War ending, if not already over? Perhaps the world was changing faster than the Berrigans and friends cared to acknowledge. After all, citizens in East Germany, Poland, and Czechoslovakia had overthrown tyrannical governments. The Berlin Wall was being dismantled. Germany would soon be reunited. Soviet troops were no longer in Afghanistan. Estonia and the Ukraine were demanding independence from the Soviet Union, and the Warsaw Pact was no longer a threat to Western Europe. The U.S. and Soviet Union had signed the INF treaty eliminating short-range atomic missiles, and another treaty eliminating some long-range missiles might soon be ratified. Indeed, many unexpected changes had taken place in the world since the Plowshare Eight walked into the General Electric plant in King of Prussia and pounded on nose cones for Mark 12-A warheads.

Unfortunately, says Philip Berrigan, "The INF Treaty was a confidence trick. It contained no provisions for dismantling of the nuclear warheads, which will be re-used. It only covered the missile casings. In the six months between signing and U.S. ratification more missiles were built in the U.S. than will be scrapped under the treaty.

"Even if the U.S. and U.S.S.R. agree to 50-percent cuts in strategic weapons (START), the destabilizing drive towards first-strike capability will remain untouched. NATO is introducing a whole new generation of nuclear weapons—Trident 11, air- and sea-launched cruise missiles, SRAM. This unilateral arms race must be stopped."[1]

It appears that the language formerly used to beguile the American people into believing our nation was locked into a life-and-death struggle with the "Evil Empire" is now being skillfully employed to convince us that the arms race is over. Thus we are waiting, say the Berrigans and friends, for the "peace dividend" to materialize, while at the White Sands proving grounds a $20-million rocket component for Star Wars research is destroyed during a test flight. We read with great expectations about superpower summits, while more Trident submarines are launched and Pentagon boondoggles continue unabated. The rhetoric once used to rationalize building missiles instead of schools, to deploy atomic weapons instead of funding hospitals, and to prepare for war rather than converting to a peacetime economy, makes little sense today. The world has changed. Our own nation's vision has not.

*        *        *

On the afternoon of April 10, 1990, people jostle, hoping to be admitted to a federal courtroom in Norristown, Pennsylvania. Lawyers, journalists, and federal marshals enter first, then relatives and close friends of the Plowshare Eight. The cheerful defiance of the previous evening is gone, replaced by the metallic reality of uniformed guards, guns, clubs, handcuffs, prosecutors with bloodshot eyes. At the back entrance to the courthouse a blue school bus, wire mesh across its windows, waits to take the Berrigans and friends to prison following resentencing. Behind the glass doors leading to the metal detector and the courtroom, guards scrutinize each spectator before allowing him or her in. People jockey for position. Some day this moment will appear in history books, and it will be good to be able to tell your children you were there.

On the grass in front of the courthouse, groups of Plowshare activists and their supporters spread picnic lunches, snap film into cameras, and scan the daily papers. Banners are unfurled on the courthouse steps. Children race about, screaming, laughing, falling. The long afternoon begins.

"I'm here," explains Plowshare activist Lin Romano, "because the Plowshare Eight changed my life, incredibly. My action was born of their action, as were hundreds after that. And I just want to support their great fortitude through the years, and their courage in breaking new ground in disarmament. What might go on in the courtroom today? Well, the only thing I know is that justice will not transpire. My guess is that the government may try to placate the peace movement by minimizing the sentences. Or the judge may even try to rein the defendants in by giving them probation. But of course that won't work. The arms race isn't over.

Preparations for war haven't ended. Invasions of other sovereign nations haven't ended. Death squads in Guatemala and El Salvador are still financed by American taxes, our own streets are still crowded with homeless, children still go to bed hungry at night, the poor still suffer, and the Pentagon continues to spend $300 billion a year, paying out taxpayers' money for $437 tape measures, $2,228 wrenches, $258 screwdrivers, and $435 hammers, for a Stealth bomber—each one costs $840 million—that will be used during a nuclear war to find targets MX and Trident missiles missed, not to mention all the weapons we insist we'll never use. So the Plowshare movement will continue, in spite of what the government does or does not say, in spite of what goes on in the courtroom today."

Max Obuszewski, personal friend of Philip Berrigan and peace activist who's been arrested more than twenty times for his support for the poor and opposition to military spending, wonders why, if the Cold War is over, researchers at colleges and universities continue to work on weapons systems.

"Among institutions of higher learning, for example, Johns Hopkins is number-two in the nation for military contracts. Last year they received $400 million in Pentagon contracts. They're the number-one Star Wars contractor in the Baltimore-Washington area, but their most heinous research is on the Trident missile. Since 1982, they've gotten over half a billion dollars to do Trident research, on the D-1 and D-2 missile. So any time a Trident submarine goes out, the black box is returned to the Johns Hopkins Applied Physics Laboratory for examination, comments, and suggestions on research and development. They're intricately tied into the

Trident missile. Any time there's a launch down at Cape Canaveral, researchers from Johns Hopkins will be there.

"I've studied slavery, and how it was finally abolished in this country. And I'm totally convinced that we, the people, will end the arms race. We'll stop the production and deployment of nuclear weapons in our own lifetime. Not because of the government. George Bush won't ever do it. I haven't seen one U.S. nuclear weapon destroyed yet. Not one since the inception of the arms race. No matter what happens inside the courthouse today, we'll keep up our efforts to disarm. And even if we do decide to reduce, or even destroy some of our nuclear weapons, that's like saying that partial slavery is all right. It wasn't. It couldn't be. It can't be. I want total, absolute abolition of our nuclear weapons. and even when that happens, there will be plenty of other weapons to destroy people with—lasers, chemical and biological agents, conventional weapons. Our work will still be cut out for us."

Inside the courthouse, Robert Jay Lifton, professor of psychiatry at Yale University, speaks about his own work with people who have survived life-threatening trauma. He tells the court about visiting Hiroshima, where he discovered that the survivors of the first atomic attack had literally stopped feeling, a phenomenon that he named "psychic numbing." Dr. Lifton explains that his work with survivors of atomic attacks, victims of the Holocaust, and Vietnam veterans has coincided through the years with the witness and work of the Berrigans and friends. The defendants, Dr. Lifton says, have made a significant contribution to waking us from our collective psychic numbing. They've done this by showing that there are really things we can do to make a difference.

Dr. Lifton also talks about a worldwide awakening, a movement toward what he terms "species consciousness," that is, the consciousness that the sufferings of anyone anywhere affect everyone everywhere. He states that the defendants have actually anticipated the direction of species consciousness, and he tells the court that to survive we must all embrace this belief.

Sister Anne Montgomery, diminutive and frail-looking, is brought into and taken out of the courtroom in handcuffs; she is currently in prison for taking part in the Thames River Plowshare action. She explains that while Ramsey Clark, Robert Jay Lifton, Howard Zinn, and other expert witnesses have helped her to better understand what she's always felt on some deep level, her real source of inspiration is "neither international laws, nor history, but the word of God. It is this call of the prophets and Jesus to beat swords into plowshares which is real. Not only must we do that with the weapons, but we must do that in our own hearts as well. I'm a fearful person," Sister Montgomery continues. "I'm afraid right now. I'm afraid in jail. And I'm afraid when I do one of these actions. But the word of God explains why I'm here. I'm literally convicted by this word of God to beat swords into plowshares. And this word has led me to reflect, and to act with others."

Scanning the records before him, Judge Buckingham tells Sister Montgomery that it is apparent she has continued her activities, even after her 1980 conviction for entering the GE plant in King of Prussia.

"Do you plan to continue your actions after this resentencing?"

"Well, I *have* been upholding the law," Sister Montgomery replies. "But I hope there will be disarmament, so I won't have to."

Father Carl Kabat, in prison for more than five years for his part in the Silo Pruning Hooks Plowshare action, is also brought into and out of the courtroom in handcuffs. Father Kabat tells the court that his father and brother died this past year, and that that has "put me in touch with how fleeting life is. And I speak to you personally," Father Kabat continues. "I believe in God's kingdom on earth, and there are many beautiful and happy things. But the world is in bad shape. People are hungry, wanting truth and justice. And we have to answer this call. We can't just say that's God's job. Because it's our job."

Father Kabat talks about being deeply affected by the witness and courage of Franz Jägerstätten, an Austrian peasant beheaded by the Germans for refusing to serve in World War II, a war Jägerstätten believed to be unjust. The judge who sentenced Jägerstätten to die, says Fr. Kabat, cried when he did so. But nevertheless he did it.

Judge Buckingham asks Father Kabat if he plans to continue his opposition to war after he's released from prison. Fr. Kabat quotes a Swiss psychologist who has written that anyone who spends five years in prison is permanently scarred. "So I've been more than five years in prison, and I'm permanently scarred," Fr. Kabat says. "I'd have to give the scars some time to heal. And I would hope we would not have to do this again. But I probably would. We'll see."

Outside a fine rain is falling and the crowd has grown smaller. The resentencing hearing, Elizabeth McAlister announces, may go into the night or perhaps continue tomorrow. Another hour passes. More rain, the crowd thinning even more. At 5:30 P.M. a television truck arrives in front of the courthouse and the reporters begin unloading. They set up on the second floor, just down the hall from the court-room. More news reporters arrive trailing microphones, waving notepads and tape recorders. A guard stands next to one of the elevators, hand resting gently on the .45 on her hip. Elmer Maas, Anne Montgomery, and Carl Kabat are led, handcuffed and smiling, from the courtroom. Daniel Berri-gan stands nose to nose with a television camera. "Will you abide by the terms of the probation?" a reporter shouts. The judge has ordered the defendants not to engage in any illegal anti-war activities, in any state in the union, for the next twenty-three months.

"Well," Daniel Berrigan replies, grinning like a wise and very tired leprechaun. "I'm going to be watching President Bush very closely. It all depends on him whether I go back to the pokey or not."

In front of the courtroom, the crowd sings "Ain't Gonna Study War No More," and dances in circles. Frida Berrigan watches her father give and receive large hugs. She smiles, shakes her head, brushes a raindrop from her cheek and sighs, "My dad." Then more forcefully, "That's my dad." Philip takes her by the hand and they join the circle. It is raining hard but no one seems to mind. The "Celebration of Hope" will continue because our government, say the Ber-rigans and friends, is not beating swords into plowshares. Headlines may change, rhetoric may be revised or restyled, grand promises made, but much of every U.S. tax dollar will continue to be spent on the military. In order to save our-selves, say our leaders, we must continue to despoil our own environment, undermine our own economy, and look upon the rest of the world as a potential enemy. Somewhere, sometime, our massive arsenal of atomic weapons may be needed, if not against the Soviet Union, then against some other, as yet undetermined, Evil Empire.

Shortly before the Plowshare Eight were resentenced, the first British Plowshares action took place at the Upper Heyford U.S. Air Force Base. Wearing Mickey Mouse ears, a silhouette the protesters felt U.S. airmen would recognize and probably not shoot at, British peace activists Stephen Hancock and Mike Hutchinson hammered on the outside of an F-111 plane, then entered the cockpit and hammered on the Nuclear Weapons Control Panel. In a prepared statement, Hancock and Hutchinson explained why they had decided to engage in an act of disarmament: "For all the intergovernmental talk of disarmament, the arms race has never been so savage, especially on British soil and in British waters. Britain is effectively an aircraft carrier for the United States, available for a nuclear strike or a 'conventional' attack, such as the bombing of Libya."[2]

On March 20, 1990, three Swedish peace activists also carried out a Plowshare action, pouring blood over and pounding on weapons in a Swedish weapons factory. The action of the Plowshare Eight at General Electric's King of Prussia plant appears, in the spring of 1990, to have been the first step in an international effort to stop the designing, testing, manufacture, and deployment of weapons of war. The "disarming atmosphere" about which Daniel Berrigan spoke seems, in spite of the resistance of governments, to be spreading.

# Notes

1. Philip Berrigan, "Swedish & English Plowshares," *The New Year One*, Vol. XVII No. 2, Jonah House, Baltimore, May 1990, 8.

2. Ibid.

# *Appendixes*

# Appendix I

## Chronology of Plowshares Disarmament Actions
### September 1980–May 1989

### by Arthur J. Laffin

INTRODUCTION: On September 9, 1980, the Plowshares Eight entered a General Electric plant in King of Prussia, Pennsylvania, where the nose cones for the Mark 12A nuclear warheads were manufactured. With hammers and blood they enacted the Biblical prophecies of Isaiah (2:4) and Micah (4:3) to "beat swords into plowshares" by hammering on two of the nose cones and pouring blood on documents. They were subsequently arrested, tried, convicted, and sentenced.

Recognizing the imminent peril nuclear weapons pose for all life, other communities and individuals since the Plowshares Eight action, after a process of spiritual preparation and reflection on the Biblical imperative to "beat swords into plowshares," have symbolically yet concretely disarmed components of U.S. first-strike nuclear weapons systems: the MX, Pershing II, Cruise, Minuteman ICBMs, Trident II missiles, Trident submarines, B-52 Bombers, P-3 Orion anti-submarine aircraft, the Navstar system, the ELF communication system and nuclear-capable battleships. Combat aircraft used for military intervention have also been disarmed. Accepting full responsibility for their actions, the Plowshares activists have peacefully awaited arrest following each act.

Resonating closely with this spirit of nonviolent direct disarmament, other people, though not seeing their action arising out of the Biblical prophesy of Isaiah and Micah, have been compelled by their conscience to nonviolently disarm components of nuclear and conventional weapons.

As of May 1989, over 100 individuals have participated in 33 Plowshares and related disarmament actions. Two groups, intending to disarm nuclear weapons components, were unable to do so because of high security. In addition to the U.S., Plowshares and related disarmament actions have also occurred in Australia, Germany, Holland, and Sweden. There have been twenty-nine trials to date, mostly jury trials, all of which have ended in convictions. (Members of the Epiphany Plowshares have been tried an unprecedented five times with three ending in hung juries and mistrials.) During these trials, which have occurred in both state and federal courts, most of the defendants have represented themselves and have been assisted by legal advisers. In their defense, many have attempted to show, through personal and expert testimony, that their actions were morally and legally justified, and that their intent was to protect life, not commit a crime. However most judges have denied this testimony and have prohibited the justification/necessity defense. Those convicted for Plowshares actions have received sentences ranging from suspended sentences to 17 years in prison. This chronology briefly describes these actions and trials and states the sentence each person received.

PLOWSHARES EIGHT. September 9, 1980, Daniel Berrigan, Jesuit priest, author and poet from New York City; Philip Berrigan, father and co-founder of Jonah House in Baltimore, MD; Dean Hammer, member of the Covenant Peace Community in New Haven, CT; Elmer Maas, musician and former college teacher from New York City; Carl Kabat, Oblate priest and missionary; Anne Montgomery, Religious of the Sacred Heart sister and teacher from New York City; Molly Rush, mother and founder of the Thomas Merton Center in Pittsburgh and John Schuchardt, ex-marine, lawyer, father and member of Jonah

House, entered the General Electric Nuclear Missile Re-entry Division in King of Prussia, PA, where nose cones for the Mark 12A warheads were made. They hammered on two nose cones, poured blood on documents and offered prayers for peace. They were arrested shortly thereafter and initially charged with over ten different felony and misdemeanor counts.

In February 1981, they underwent a jury trial in Norristown, Pennsylvania. During their trial they were denied a "justification defense" and could not present expert testimony. Due to the court's suppression of individual testimony about the Mark 12A and U.S. nuclear war–fighting policies, four left the trial and returned to witness at GE. They were re-arrested and returned to court. They were convicted by a jury of burglary, conspiracy and criminal mischief and sentenced to prison terms of five to ten years. They appealed and the Pennsylvania Superior Court reversed their conviction in February 1984. The State of Pennsylvania then appealed that decision. Following a ruling in the fall of 1985 by the Pennsylvania Supreme Court in favor of the state on certain issues (including the exclusion of the justification defense), the case has been returned to the Superior Court Appeals Panel. In December of 1987, the Superior Court of Pennsylvania refused their appeal, but ordered a resentencing.

In February 1989, the Pennsylvania Supreme Court denied a hearing of any further issues in the case and ordered resentencing of the defendants. A motion to stay the sentencing, pending a final appeal to the U.S. Supreme Court, was granted in late March. The Plowshares Eight were resentenced on April 10, 1990.

PLOWSHARES NUMBER TWO. On December 13, 1980, Peter De-Mott, former seminarian and Vietnam veteran from Jonah House, entered the General Dynamics Electric Boat (EB) shipyard in Groton, Connecticut, during the launch ceremony for the USS *Baltimore* fast-attack submarine. Noticing an empty EB security van with keys in it, he got into the van and repeatedly rammed the Trident USS *Florida*, denting the rudder. Security guards then broke into the van and arrested him. Conducting his own defense during a weeklong jury trial, he was convicted of criminal mischief and criminal trespass and sentenced to one year in jail.

TRIDENT NEIN. Independence Day, 1982, Judy Beaumont, a Benedictine sister and teacher from Chicago; Anne Montgomery, of the Plowshares Eight; James Cunningham, an ex-lawyer from Jonah House; George Veasey, a Vietnam veteran also from Jonah House; Tim Quinn, expectant father and housepainter from Hartford, CT; Anne Bennis, teacher from Philadelphia; Bill Hartman, peace worker from Philadelphia; Vincent Kay, housepainter and poet from New Haven, and Art Laffin, member of the Covenant Peace Community in New Haven, entered EB to make a "declaration of independence" from the Trident submarine and all nuclear weapons. Four boarded the Trident USS *Florida* by canoe, hammered on several missile hatches, poured blood, and with spray paint renamed the submarine USS *Auschwitz*. They were arrested within half an hour. Meanwhile, five others entered EB's south storage yard and hammered and poured blood on two Trident sonar spheres. They were apprehended after three hours. During their two week jury trial, they were disallowed a justification defense and expert witnesses were prohibited from testifying about the dangers of the first-strike Trident. They were convicted of criminal mischief, conspiracy, and criminal trespass and ordered to pay $1,386.67 in restitution to the Navy. They were sentenced to jail for up to one year.

PLOWSHARES NUMBER FOUR. November 14, 1982—five days after the Trident Nein sentencing—John Grady, auto mechanic from Ithaca, New York; Ellen Grady, aide to an elderly woman and peace worker, also from Ithaca; Peter DeMott, of Plowshares Number Two; Jean Holladay, grandmother and nurse from Massachusetts; Roger Ludwig, a poet and musician involved in work with the poor in Washington, D.C.; Elmer Maas, of the Plowshares Eight, and Marcia Timmel, from the Dorothy Day Catholic Worker in Washington, D.C., entered EB. Three boarded the Trident USS *Georgia* and hammered and poured blood on several missile hatches. Four others entered the south storage yard and poured blood and hammered on Trident components before being quickly apprehended. Like the Trident Nein, they underwent a jury trial and were denied a justification defense. They also were convicted of criminal mischief, conspiracy, and criminal trespass. They received prison sentences ranging from two months to one year.

AVCO PLOWSHARES. July 14, 1983, Agnes Bauerlein, mother and grandmother from Ambler, PA; Macy Morse, mother and grandmother from Nashua, NH; Mary Lyons, mother, grandmother, and teacher from Hartford, CT; Frank Panopoulos, member of the Cor Jesu community from New York City; Jean Holladay, of the Plowshares Number Four; John Pendleton, member of Jonah House and John Schuchardt, of the Plowshares Eight, entered the AVCO Systems Division in Wilmington, Massachusetts, where MX and Pershing II nuclear weapons components are produced. They hammered on computer equipment related to these weapons systems and poured blood on blueprints labeled "MX-Peacekeeper." They also served AVCO and its co-conspirators, including the national security state and the armed forces, with an indictment for committing crimes against God and humanity by manufacturing for profit weapons of genocide. They were apprehended within an hour. During their jury trial they were able to present a justification defense but this defense and expert testimony was disallowed by the judge prior to jury deliberation. They were convicted of wanton destruction and trespass. They were sentenced to jail for up to three-and-a-half months. They appealed this decision.

GRIFFISS PLOWSHARES. Thanksgiving Day, November 24, 1983, Jackie Allen, a nursery school teacher from Hartford, CT; Clare Grady, an artist and potter from Ithaca, NY; Dean Hammer, father and member of the Plowshares Eight; Elizabeth McAlister, mother and co-founder of Jonah House; Vern Rossman, minister, father, and grandfather from Boston, MA; Kathleen Rumpf, a Catholic worker from Marlboro, NY and Karl Smith, member of Jonah House, entered Griffiss Air Force Base in Rome, NY. They hammered and poured blood on a B-52 bomber converted to carry cruise missiles, and on B-52 engines. They left at the site of their witness a written indictment of Griffiss Air Force Base and the U.S. government, pointing to the war crimes of preparing for nuclear war and depicting how the new state religion of "nuclearism" denies constitutional rights and punishes acts of conscience. Unnoticed for several hours, they finally approached security guards and were arrested.

In this, the first Plowshares case to be tried in federal court, the justification defense was denied. They were acquitted by a jury of sabotage, but they were convicted of conspiracy and destruction of government property. They received prison sentences ranging from two to three years. Their appeal was denied in federal court in March 1985.

PLOWSHARES NUMBER SEVEN. On December 4, 1983, Carl Kabat of the Plowshares Eight and three West Germans—Herwig Jantschik, Dr. Wolfgang Sternstein, and Karin Vix—entered a U.S. Army base in Schwabisch-Gmund, West Germany, and carried out the first Plowshares action in Europe. Six weeks earlier, they had publicly announced their action, but did not disclose the exact date or place. They participated in a six-week peace march in Germany, where they distributed a booklet informing the public and media about their action and previous Plowshares actions. On December 4, they entered the base early in the morning and with hammers and bolt-cutters disarmed a Pershing II missile launcher. They were soon apprehended by U.S. soldiers. Following their arrest, they were all released ROR. Carl returned to the U.S. and did not attend the trial. During the first week of February 1985, the three Germans were tried before the three judges and two lay judges and convicted. After their conviction, the judges called the Pershing II a "bad prophesy," and characterized their action as violence. Herwig and Wolfgang were sentenced to 1800 dm ($900) or 90 days in jail, while Karin was sentenced to 450 dm ($225) or 60 days in jail. Karin and Herwig served their prison sentence; Wolfgang paid the fine.

PERSHING PLOWSHARES. In the season of Passover, Easter Morning, April 22, 1984, Per Herngren, a student and peace worker from Sweden; Paul Magno, from the Dorothy Day Catholic Worker in Washington, D.C.; Todd Kaplan, involved in work with the poor in Washington, D.C.; Tim Lietzke, member of Jeremiah House in Richmond, VA; Anne Montgomery, of the Plowshares Eight and Trident Nein; Patrick O'Neill, university student and peace worker from Greenville, North Carolina; Jim Perkins, teacher, father, and member of Jonah House; and Christin Schmidt, university student and peace worker from Rhode Island, entered Martin Marietta in Orlando, Florida. Once inside, they hammered and poured blood on Pershing II missile components and on a Patriot missile launcher. They served Martin Marietta with an indictment for engaging in the criminal activity of building nuclear weapons in violation of divine, international, and national law. They also displayed a banner which said: VIOLENCE ENDS WHERE LOVE BEGINS. They were apprehended after several hours. During their jury trial in Federal Court they were denied a justification defense. They were convicted of depredation of government property and conspiracy. They were sentenced to three years in federal prison, given five years suspended sentences with probation, and each ordered to pay $2900 in restitution. Both their appeal and motion for reduction of sentence has been denied in federal court. Herngren, a Swedish national, was deported on August 27, 1985, after serving over a year of his sentence. The other seven have served their sentences and remain on probation through 1991.

SPERRY SOFTWARE PAIR. August 10, 1984, John LaForge and Barbara Katt, house-painters and peace workers from Bemidji, MN, dressed as quality-control inspectors, entered Sperry Corporation in Eagan, Minnesota. Once inside they poured blood and hammered on two prototype computers designed to provide guidance and navigation information for Trident submarines and F4G fighter bombers. In addressing Sperry's nuclear-war preparations, they also served Sperry with a citizens' indictment declaring that they are committing war crimes in violation of national and international law. After a two-day jury trial in federal court in which they were allowed to present a justification defense, they were convicted of destruction of government property. Judge Miles Lord imposed a six-month suspended sentence and used the occasion to criticize the arms industry, and to cite Sperry's corporate corruption. He also recognized the legitimacy of the justification defense for civil disobedience trials and for the Sperry Software trial in particular.

TRIDENT II PLOWSHARES. October 1, 1984, William Boston, a house painter and peace worker from New Haven, CT; Jean Holladay, of the Plowshares Number Four and AVCO Plowshares; Frank Panopoulos and John Pendleton of the AVCO Plowshares, and Leo Schiff, draft registration resister and natural foods chef from Vermont, entered the EB Quonset Point facility in North Kingston, Rhode Island. They hammered and poured blood on six Trident II missile tubes and unfurled a banner which said: HARVEST OF HOPE—SWORDS INTO PLOWSHARES. They placed a pumpkin at the site and posted a written Call to Conscience on the missile tubes condemning these weapons under international and religious law and calling on those responsible to cease their crimes against humanity. They were arrested within half an hour and charged with possession of burglary tools, malicious damage to property and criminal trespass.

During their jury trial, expert witnesses were allowed to be qualified in the presence of the jury. However the judge ruled this and other expert testimony irrelevant and denied a justification defense. At the end of their two-week-long trial, the prosecution dropped the burglary tools charge (a felony carrying ten years) as the defendants pled guilty to the malicious damage to property charge. (After the state's case, the judge dismissed the trespass charge.) After two days of prayer and discernment, the five concluded that pleading guilty was the most nonviolent course to take. On October 18, 1985, they were each sentenced to one year and a $500 fine. Frank was given an additional two months for a contempt charge relating to his refusal to disclose to the judge who drove the group to EB. All five served their sentences and were released by October 1986.

SILO PRUNING HOOKS. November 12, 1984, Carl Kabat, of the Plowshares Eight and Plowshares Number Seven; Paul Kabat, an Oblate priest from Minnesota; Larry Cloud Morgan, Native American and mental health care worker from Minneapolis, MN; Helen Woodson, mother of eleven children and founder of the Gaudete Peace and Justice Center from Madison, WI, entered a Minuteman II missile silo controlled by Whiteman Air Force Base in Knob Noster, Missouri. Once inside the silo area, they used a jackhammer and air-compressor to damage the silo cover lid. They then offered a Eucharist and left at the silo a Biblical and Native American indictment of the U.S. government and the institutional church for their complicity in the pending omnicide of nuclear holocaust. They were arrested close to an hour after their action by armed military guards authorized to use deadly force against intruders. (As has been the case in each of the Plowshares actions, nobody was harmed.) Following their arrest, they were declared by the court to be a threat to the community and were thus held on preventive detention and denied bond.

They underwent a jury trial in Federal Court in February 1985 in Kansas City, Missouri. They were convicted of destruction of government property, conspiracy, intent to damage the national defense and trespass. On March 27, 1985, they received the most severe prison sentences to date of any Plowshares group: Larry, eight years; Paul, ten years; and Carl and Helen, eighteen years. They were also given three to five years probation and ordered to pay $2,932.80 each in restitution. They are now serving their sentences and all but Helen have appealed their case, which was denied in federal court in the spring of 1986. On November 1, 1985, U.S. District Judge D. Brook Bartlett, their trial judge, reduced Helen's sentence from eighteen to twelve years, including 5 years probation. In March 1987, Larry and Paul were released from prison following a sentence reduction hearing. Larry's sentence was reduced to 36 months and three years probation while Paul's sentence was reduced to 40 months and 4 years probation. All but Helen have appealed their case, which was denied in the spring of 1986. On April 22, 1987, the U.S. Supreme Court ruled not to consider Carl's appeal. His sentence has since been reduced to ten years, including five years probation.

On March 16, 1988, Helen Woodson walked through the main gate of Alderson Prison carrying a banner and statement, protesting the nuclear arms race, pollution of the environment, and prison conditions for women. She was apprehended outside the prison by a patrol vehicle. She was temporarily placed in solitary confinement and then transferred to FCI Pleasanton in California. On December 10, 1988, in honor of Gaudete (Rejoice!) Sunday, Helen carried out another resistance action, this time, at FCI Pleasanton. She walked to the rec field track bearing an athletic bag stuffed with sheets, towels and papers doused with flammable nail polish, set the bag next to the fence and ignited a "lovely advent blaze." Then she hung a banner reading: "There is no security in the U.S. government, nuclear weapons, chemical contaminants, prisons, and UNICOR-military prison industries. Fences make slaves. Tear Them Down." And then with toenail clippers, she snipped the security alarm wire, severing it in four separate places. She was sent to the hole and charged with attempted escape, arson, destruction of government property, and inciting to riot. In late January 1989 she was moved to MCC San Diego.

On January 27, 1989 Larry Cloud Morgan was convicted of two counts of going out of the district of Minnesota, a violation of his probation, and was sentenced to prison for one year. The occasions of his departures were to attend protests at the Trident base in King's Bay, Georgia. He was taken into custody by U.S. marshalls at a church near the Trident base. Due to health reasons, the judge recommended that Larry be sent to the Medical Center for Federal Prisoners in Rochester, Minnesota.

PLOWSHARES NUMBER TWELVE. February 19, 1985, Martin Holladay, a carpenter from Sheffield, Vermont, entered another Minuteman II missile silo at Whiteman Air Force Base, near Odessa, Missouri. He damaged the lid of the silo with a hammer and chisel, along with some electrical boxes. He also poured blood on the silo and spray-painted "No More Hiroshimas." He left at the site an indictment charging the U.S. government with committing crimes against God and international law by its nuclear-war preparations. After his arrest, he was denied bond and held until trial. During his four-day jury trial, he was denied the opportunity to present a justification defense. On April 25, 1985, he was convicted of destruction of government property and destruction of national defense material. He was sentenced on May 16, 1985, to eight years in federal prison and five years probation. He was also fined $1,000 and ordered to pay $2,242 in restitution. Martin was released from prison after 19 months following a sentence reduction hearing on September 24, 1986. He remains on probation through 1991 and is required to pay restitution and not violate the law during his probation.

TRIDENT II PRUNING HOOKS. April 18, 1985, Greg Boertje, ex–army officer and peace organizer from Louisiana; John Heid, former Franciscan seminarian and social worker from Ithaca, NY; Roger Ludwig, of the Plowshares Number Four; Sheila Parks, former college teacher from Medford, MA; Suzanne Schmidt, mother, grandmother, worker with the disabled, and member of Jonah House; and George Veasey, of the Trident Nein, entered the EB Quonset Point facility in North Kingston, Rhode Island—the same site where the Trident II Plowshares had acted seven months earlier. They poured blood and hammered on three Trident II missile tubes and spraypainted "Dachau" on them. They left there a "Call to Conscience" indicting General Dynamics for war crimes and preparing for a war of aggression in violation of international, constitutional and spiritual law. They were also able to celebrate a Jewish-Christian ceremony of faith and hope. Arrested after a short time, they were charged with possession of burglary tools, malicious damage to property and criminal trespass and held on $18,000 bond. While Sheila and Suzanne were released nearly a month after the action on a "Promise to Appear" (PTA) and John after five months, Greg, George, and Roger remained in jail for nearly nine months, refusing to accept a PTA for reasons of conscience. Shortly before their trail date, the judge released the three unconditionally from prison. During their two-week jury trial, the judge denied their justification defense, insisting that their motives were irrelevant to the case. They were convicted of all three charges. (In a special gesture of support for the group, four jurors had the judge publicly read a statement from them that they were sympathetic to their cause.) On March 31, 1986, they were sentenced to three years, suspended after one year, and given two years probation. Greg, Suzanne, and Sheila are appealing their case. John, Greg, George, and Roger were released during the summer of 1986. Sheila and Suzanne were released in January 1987.

MICHIGAN ELF DISARMAMENT ACTION. May 28, 1985, Tom Hastings, a peace activist involved in radio work from Wisconsin, entered a wooded area in Michigan's upper peninsula and sawed down one of the poles carrying the Navy's "Extremely Low Frequency" (ELF) transmitter antennas which are used to coordinate the communications, command, and control process of all nuclear submarines in the U.S. He remained at the site for 45 minutes, praying, singing and planting a circle of corn around the pole. The next morning, he gave a part of the pole to Congressman Bob Davis's office and turned himself in to the local sheriff. Held for 48 hours, he was released on personal recognizance. He underwent a jury trial and was convicted of malicious destruction of property. On September 27, 1985, he was sentenced to fifteen days and two years probation.

PANTEX DISARMAMENT ACTION. July 16, 1985, Richard Miller, involved in work with the poor in Des Moines, Iowa, began dismantling a section of railroad track from the railroad spur leading from U.S. Department of Energy's Pantex Nuclear Weapons Assembly Plant in Amarillo, Texas, to a main line of the Topeka and Santa Fe Railroad. After first taking extensive precautions to prevent accidental derailment and avoid personal injury, he labored with railroad tools for seven hours, removing a 39-foot section of rail. Pointing out the connection between the Nazi extermination camp at Auschwitz and the Pantex factory, which is the final assembly point for every nuclear weapon made in the U.S., he put up a banner that read: PANTEX = AUSCHWITZ—STOP THE TRAINS. He further stated: "At Auschwitz the trains carried the people to the crematoria; at Pantex the trains carry the crematoria to the people." Charged with wrecking trains and destruction of national defense materials, he underwent a jury trial in federal court and was convicted. On November 8, 1985, he was sentenced to two four-year sentences to run concurrently. He was released from prison in February 1989 upon completing his sentence.

WISCONSIN ELF DISARMAMENT ACTION. August 14, 1985, Jeff Leys, a draft registration resister and peace worker from St. Paul, Minnesota, continued the process of disarming ELF (see Michigan ELF action) by sawing two deep notches in an ELF pole hoping to weaken it and leaving the rest to natural forces. (Unlike the Michigan ELF, still under construction, the 56-mile Wisconsin ELF system is fully operational, with 1.5 million watts flowing through it.) In a statement he carried with him to the site he explained: "I act today in accordance with the teachings of Gandhi, Christ, and the Indians—and in accordance with the basic underpinnings of humanity, as expressed in the various world religions . . . and international laws." After an hour, Jeff walked to a transmitter site to turn himself in. Jailed after his arrest, he was tried by a jury on September 30, 1985 and was convicted of criminal damage to property. On October 29, 1985, Jeff was sentenced to five months in jail and given a three years suspended sentence with three years probation. He was also ordered to pay $4,775 in restitution. In April of 1986 Jeff began serving his three-year sentence because of his refusal to pay restitution for reasons of conscience. His appeal was denied in September 1986. He was released in August 1987.

MARTIN MARIETTA MX WITNESS. September 27, 1985, Al Zook, father and grandfather active with the Catholic Worker in Denver, CO; Mary Sprunger-Froese, member of the Bijou Community and involved in hospitality work in Colorado Springs, CO; and Marie Nord, a Minnesota Franciscan sister involved in hospitality work for women, entered Martin Marietta's Denver, Colorado, plant. (Martin Marietta has a $2 billion contract for building and testing the MX missile.) With the intent of disarming components of the MX missile, they carried blood and hammers into the MX work area. Finding the area highly secured by employees wearing "peacekeeper" security badges, the three were not able to enter areas where MX work is done and directly disarm any MX components. They were, however, able to pour blood on large interior windows overlooking the work area and unfurled their banner: SWORDS INTO PLOWSHARES. They were quickly arrested and each charged with felony burglary and criminal mischief. The burglary charge was eventually dropped, but the criminal mischief charge was changed from a misdemeanor to a felony. They were imprisoned for one month before they were released on their own recognizance. On March 5, 1986, they were found guilty by a jury of criminal mischief exceeding $300. During their trial the judge refused to hear their justification defense. On May 1, 1986, they were sentenced to two months in prison.

Al and Marie appealed their case and the Colorado Court of Appeals recently reversed their convictions. The appeal was based on the judge's denial of their motion to proceed *in forma pauperis*, after his determination that their indigency was voluntary. The state has petitioned for a review of the case before deciding to retry Al and Marie.

SILO PLOWSHARES. Good Friday, March 28, 1986, Darla Bradley and Larry Morlan of the Davenport Catholic Worker in Iowa; Jean Gump, a mother of twelve and grandmother from Morton Grove, Illinois; Ken Rippetoe, a member of the Catholic Worker in Rock Island, Illinois; and John Volpe, father, former employee at the Rock Island Arsenal and member of the Davenport Catholic Worker, entered two Minuteman Missile Silos controlled by Whiteman Air Force Base near Holden, Missouri. Dividing into two groups, the first group of three went to Silo M10 while the second group went to Silo M6. Hanging banners on the silo fences, one of which read: DISARMAMENT—AN ACT OF HEALING they employed sledgehammers to split and disarm the geared central track used to move the 120 ton missile silo cover at the time of launch. They also cut circuits and used masonry hammers to damage electrical sensor equipment. They then poured blood on the silo covers in the form of a cross and spraypainted "Disarm and Live" and "For the Children" on the silo pad. They left at the site an indictment charging the U.S. government with committing crimes against the laws of God and humanity and indicting as well the institutional Christian church for its complicity in the arms race. They were arrested nearly 40 minutes after their action by heavily armed military police. Following their arrest they were taken into custody and then released on their own recognizance. During their five-day jury trial they presented important evidence regarding their state of mind but the jury was not allowed to consider justification as a defense. On June 27, 1986, they were convicted of destruction of government property and conspiracy. In addition, Jean, Larry, and Darla were cited for contempt for refusing to answer questions about where they met prior to the action. They served seven days in jail following the trial. John and Ken were also imprisoned for refusing to cooperate with the conditions of their release so long as the others were imprisoned for contempt. They were released on July 8. On August 22, 1986, Darla, Jean, Ken and Larry were sentenced to eight years with five years probation while John was sentenced to seven years with five years probation. John and Darla were ordered to pay $1,680 in restitution while Larry, Jean, and Ken were ordered to pay $424. Each was also fined $100.

In April 1987, John was released from prison following a sentence reduction hearing. His sentence was reduced to ten months, five years probation, and he is required to pay restitution. Ken and Darla were released from prison in mid-June 1987 after their sentence was reduced to one year. They remain on probation for five years and are required to pay restitution. All are required not to violate the law for the duration of their probation. Jean and Larry are currently serving their sentences which have been reduced to six years and five years probation. In March of 1989, Jean was placed in solitary confinement for refusing a urine test in the presence of guards.

PERSHING TO PLOWSHARES. On December 12, 1986, on the seventh anniversary of the NATO decision to deploy the cruise and Pershing II in Europe, Heike Huschauer, a member of the city council of Neuss, West Germany; Suzanne Mauch-Friz, a social worker from Stuttgart; Wolfgang Sternstein, Plowshares Number Seven; and Stellan Vinthagen, an orderly from Sweden, entered a back-up U.S. Army weapons depot at Schwabisch-Gmund, West Germany, and damaged the tractor-rig of a Pershing II Missile Launch box. They hammered on the crane that maneuvers the missile and on the generator that operates the launcher; and poured blood on the rig. The banner which they hung over the truck stated, CHOOSE LIFE FOR THE CHILDREN AND POOR. These words were also spraypainted on the road way. They were discovered after thirty minutes, when they signalled to a nearby guard.

In a statement of intent the four said, "With awareness of our responsibility we understand that we are the ones who make the arms race possible by not trying to stop it." Following their arrest, they were released. Their case is still unresolved.

EPIPHANY PLOWSHARES. On January 6, 1987, the Christian Feast of Epiphany, Greg Boertje, of the Trident II Pruning Hooks; Rev. Dexter Lanctot and Rev. Thomas McGann, priests of the Archdiocese of Philadelphia, and Lin Romano, an advocate for the poor from Washington D.C., entered the Willow Grove Naval Air Station in Horsham, PA. Dividing into two groups, one group went to a Navy P-3 Orion antisubmarine aircraft—an essential part of the U.S. first-strike arsenal. Meanwhile the other group went to a Marine CH-53 Sea Stallion and an Army H-1 Huey helicopter—both integral parts of U.S. interventionary forces. Both groups hammered and poured blood on the aircraft and displayed banners which proclaimed: SEEK THE DISARMED CHRIST and ESPADAS EN ARADOS—SWORDS INTO PLOWSHARES. The four left behind a statement which explained why they acted on Epiphany, the

Christian feast that recalls the three Magi's search for the Christ child, "who came in the name of Peace." Having therefore addressed the "deadly connection" between nuclear weapons and military intervention, they also left an indictment of the US government for its "criminal interventionary" wars in Central America and the Middle East and its "first-strike nuclear war making policies." They were charged with conspiracy, destruction of government property and trespass, charges which carry up to fifteen years.

On March 31, they underwent a weeklong jury trial in federal court in Philadelphia and were prevented from presenting a crime prevention or necessity defense. For the first time in a Plowshares case, the trial ended in a hung jury and a mistrial. On May 11, 1987 they were retried. The defendants were once again denied their affirmative defenses and their testimony was even more severely restricted than in the first trial. Despite the constraints of the court, their trial once again ended in a hung jury and a mistrial. In an interview following the trial, one juror stated he believed the group did not act with criminal intent and affirmed their efforts for disarmament. After the second trial the two priests, who were suspended from their priestly duties after the action, accepted a plea bargain, pled guilty to criminal trespass, and were sentenced to 100 days in federal prison plus $500 fines. Their suspensions were lifted following their release from prison.

On July 13, 1987, a third trial began for Boertje and Romano. This trial ended in a mistrial when the judge ruled that the jury had been "contaminated" by statements from the defendants and spectators which included forbidden topics such as international law. On September 21, 1987, a fourth trial began. The judge's repressive "gag order" remained in effect. During the trial, both defendants received two contempt charges and had lawyers appointed to represent them (defendants had been representing themselves). On September 25, 1987, they were found guilty of all three charges.

On November 17, Lin was sentenced to two years and 100 days in prison plus five years probation. For reasons of conscience, Greg chose not to appear for sentencing. In a written public statement issued at the time of sentencing, Greg stated his intention to go "underground" and eventually emerge in another non-violent action.

Following his trial, conviction, and sentencing for the Nuclear Navy Plowshares action, Greg was sentenced to thirty-three months for failing to appear at the original sentencing for the Epiphany action. Lin, and then Greg, appealed their cases from prison on the grounds that the judge violated their *pro se* rights when he appointed lawyers to represent them. They won the appeal and each was granted individual trials. Lin was eventually released from prison after serving nine months. In November 1988 her charges were reduced to trespass, whereby she is not entitled to a jury trial. She was tried before a U.S. Magistrate, convicted, and was sentenced to six months probation, even though she had already served more jail time than the maximum sentence for trespass: six months.

In April 1989 charges against Greg were dropped, though he still remains in prison serving a thirty-three-month sentence for failure to appear at sentencing. Imprisoned at Oakdale SCI, Greg was recently sent to the hole for participating in a food strike with other prisoners to protest overcrowded prison conditions.

PAUPERS PLOWSHARES. On Good Friday, April 17, 1987, two brothers, Father Pat Sieber, a Franciscan priest who works at St. Francis Inn, a shelter for the homeless and soup kitchen in Philadelphia, and Rick Sieber, a father of three who also works at St. Francis Inn, entered the Naval Air Development Center in Warminster, PA. Once inside, they dug a hole and buried a foot-long coffin that listed the names of 65 homeless and poor people who have been buried in an unkept lot in northeast Philadelphia known as potter's or "paupers" field since 1980. They placed a three-foot cross bearing the same names on top of the makeshift grave. They then approached a P-3 Orion aircraft, an integral part of the U.S. first-strike arsenal, and hammered on the plane's strobe light, cut wires on the nose of the plane, and poured blood on a wing and fuselage area of the aircraft. While awaiting arrest they knelt in prayer and held a banner which said: GOD HEARS THE CRY OF THE POOR. They left at the site a statement and indictment addressing the criminality of U.S. nuclear war preparations, the priority the government gives to arms over the poor, and how these arms preparations are actually killing the poor. In addition to signing their own names to these statements, they also signed the name "Lazarus" to represent the poor for whom they acted. They were arrested after a half an hour and charged with unlawful entry and destruction of government property. On June 12, the charges were reduced to one misdemeanor—unlawful entry.

On August 5, 1987, after an hourlong bench trial, the pair were found guilty of unlawful entry. They were sentenced to one year's probation, fined $100 and ordered to pay $1,540 in restitution. In February 1989 their restitution was dropped and they paid their fine, which went towards a victims' compensation fund.

WHITE ROSE DISARMAMENT ACTION. On June 2, 1987, in the early morning, Kạtya Komisaruk, a peace activist from the San Francisco Bay area, walked through an unlocked gate leaving cookies and a bouquet of flowers for security guards and entered a satellite control facility named NAVSTAR at the Vandenberg Air Force Base in Santa Barbara County, California. 'NAVSTAR' is the U.S. global positioning system of satellites. When fully operational in 1991, this system will consist of eighteen orbiting satellites which will be able to provide the navigational and guidance signals to Trident II and other nuclear missiles as well as the Star Wars system, for a first-strike nuclear attack.

Once inside, she used a hammer, crowbar and cordless electric drill to damage panels of an IBM mainframe computer and a satellite dish on top of the building. Using a crowbar she removed the computer's chip boards and danced on them. On the walls she spray-painted "Nuremberg," "International Law," and statements for disarmament. After being undetected for two hours, she left the base and hitchhiked to San Francisco. The next morning she held a press conference at the Federal Building in San Francisco to explain her action whereupon she was taken into custody by the FBI. She was charged with injury to national defense materials (sabotage). Each charge carries a maximum penalty of ten years in prison and/or a $250,000 fine. The day before her trial the sabotage charge was dropped in the face of a defense brief that had been earlier submitted calling upon the government to prove every element of the charge beyond a reasonable doubt. Her trial began on November 10, 1987 in Los Angeles Federal Court. Several weeks before the trial, Judge Rea ruled in favor of the U.S. prosecutor's *motion in limine* which would severely restrict the evidence allowed as well as Katya's personal testimony. Katya, who represented herself and was assisted by co-counsel, was not allowed to mention words like "nuclear missiles" or "first-strike." The jury found her guilty of destruction of property on November 16, 1987. On January 11, 1988 Katya was sentenced to 5 years in prison. In addition Judge Rea ordered her to pay $500,000 restitution because he had heard that there might be a movie or book based on her action. Katya closely identifies with Sophie Scholl, a young German woman and member of the White Rose group during World War II, who was executed by the Third Reich for publicly opposing Nazi atrocities.

TRANSFIGURATION PLOWSHARES (WEST). On August 5, 1987, at 5:15 P.M., the exact moment (8:15 A.M. in Japan) when the U.S. dropped the first atomic bomb on Hiroshima in 1945, Jerry Ebner, a member of the Catholic Worker Community of Milwaukee; Joe Gump, father of twelve and husband of the imprisoned Jean Gump of the Silo Plowshares from Morton Grove, Ill.; and Helen Woodson, acting as a "co-conspirator" from Shakopee Prison in Minnesota where she was serving a seventeen-year sentence for the Silo Pruning Hooks action, carried out the fourth nonviolent disarmament of a Minuteman missile silo controlled by Whiteman AFB in Missouri. They went to silo K-9 near Butler, Missouri, and once inside the silo area Jerry and Joe locked themselves within the fenced-in area with a Kryptonite bicycle lock. After pouring their own blood in the shape of a cross on the concrete silo lid, they used one eight-and-one three-pound sledge hammer on the tracks used to open the silo lid. They hammered on electrical connectors and other apparatus and cut various electric wires with bolt cutters. They then hung disarmament banners and gathered in prayer and song to await arrest. They also left at the site of their action a statement and indictment which was signed by the three, as well as a photo of Jerry, Joe, and Helen. In the interest of "conservation," they used the very same banners and bolt cutters used by the Silo Pruning Hooks and Silo Plowshares. A while later, military police arrived in a vehicle armed with a machine gun and arrested Jerry and Joe. At no time did the two endanger anyone or the missile warhead.

Explaining her involvement in the action, Helen stated she participated "in spirit" through a "conspiracy for life." The three named themselves the "Transfiguration Plowshares" to commemorate the Transfiguration, the Christian feast celebrated on August 6 which recalls the revelation of Christ to his disciples as the Lord of heaven and earth and also represents a foreshadowing of Christ's resurrection.

At a mid-August court hearing, they were charged with a two-count felony indictment: conspiring to damage government property and destruction of government property—both federal charges. In a relatively open trial, the two were allowed to show a video film entitled *Hiroshima/Nagasaki: 1945*. This video, which the two carried into the silo with them, contained footage of the immediate effect of the bomb dropped on the two cities. Jerry was able to sing two songs to the jury which he first sang at the silo. Judge Howard Sachs, however, made it clear in his instructions to the jury that these things were ultimately irrelevant to the case before them. On October 22, the jury found them guilty. On December 11, 1987 Jerry Ebner and Joe Gump were sentenced to forty and thirty months respectively in prison.

TRANSFIGURATION PLOWSHARES (EAST). On August 6, 1987, Hiroshima Day and the Christian feast of the Transfiguration, Margaret Brodhead, a journalist; Dan Ethier, a former computer programmer and Catholic Worker; and Tom Lewis, artist and longtime peace activist—all from Worcester, MA—entered the South Weymouth Naval Air Station near Boston at dawn. They hammered and poured blood on the bomb-bay doors and bomb racks of a P-3 Orion nuclear-capable anti-submarine plane which can use nuclear depth charges and homing torpedoes to attack submarines. They hammered as well on the magnetic anomaly detector of an S-H2F LAMPS MK-1 Sea Sprite helicopter. These same types of aircraft are currently deployed by U.S. forces in the Persian Gulf and are an integral part of U.S. offensive anti-submarine warfare strategy which allows the Navy to project force in the Middle East as well as Central America.

They hung pictures of Hiroshima victims on the aircraft as well as a "Swords Into Plowshares" banner. In a signed statement and indictment they left at the site, they said "the blinding light of that first atomic bomb turned life into death, but the blinding light of the Transfiguration revealed that death would be turned into life in Christ's Resurrection." They further charged the "Nuclear National Security State" with contravening international and divine laws. They were taken into custody by base security shortly after their action as they knelt in prayer holding a banner that read CHRIST TRANSFIGURED—DEATH INTO LIFE.

The three were initially charged with unlawful entry, a federal misdemeanor. In December, Dan plead no contest and was sentenced to six months probation and community service of 100 hours. Tom and Meg were convicted on March 4, 1988, after a six-hour bench trial in Boston, where they presented testimony on the unconstitutional status of the arms race and the aircraft's status as "instrumentalities of crime" under international law. On April 26, Meg and Tom were sentenced to six months probation and 100 hours community service.

HARMONIC DISARMAMENT FOR LIFE. On August 16, 1987, the day of Harmonic Convergence, George Ostensen, a peace activist from the Northeast, in conspiracy with Plowshares prisoner Helen Woodson, enacted a Plowshares action at the ELF Communication System Transmitter Site near Clam Lake, Wisconsin. Early in the morning, George entered the North ground of the ELF Trident communication system. Using a hatchet, saw, and other tools, he proceeded to cut down three ELF poles, spraypainted disarmament slogans on them, notched two other poles, and cut some ground wires. He poured blood over the poles, hammered on groundwell electrical control boxes, and poured blood and ashes inside them. He also placed photos of children and planted flowers inside the boxes and near the poles. He spraypainted DISARM FIRST STRIKE inside the boxes and hung peace banners.

In statements he carried on to the site, George stated: "I act at the ELF Trident communication system in an attempt to stop these deadly messages from being transmitted. These Extremely Low Frequencies hurt our earth by subjecting all God's creatures to highly unstable electromagnetic non-ionizing radiation and giving the Trident first-strike capability to destroy all life." In reference to the harmonic convergence, the lining up of the planets on August 15 and 16, he stated the convergence is the beginning of the new age, the age of change, movement, spiritual consciousness, and harmony according to ancient Mayan, Tibetan, and Hopi calendars.

Following his action at the North Ground, George, undetected, went to the Terminal Control Center to inform the security guards on duty of his action. After spray-painting on the terminal center TRIDENT—ELF IS IN VIOLATION OF INTERNATIONAL LAW AND GOD'S LAW and SWORDS INTO PLOWSHARES, he spoke with a security guard who asked him to leave the site. George then went to a fenced-in area near the control center and manually switched off several generators used to control computers and electricity at the site. This happened on three separate occasions following each time George informed security personnel that the ELF site must be shut down because it is in violation of the law. Finally, the local sheriff was called and George was arrested—some nine hours after he entered the site.

In an indictment issued in state court on August 20, George was charged with two felony counts of sabotage, both state charges and each carrying a maximum penalty of ten years in prison if convicted. The indictment listed Helen as aiding and abetting the action and noted the ELF site had to be closed for twenty-nine hours. On January 10, 1988, George was convicted of one count of sabotage and acquitted on the second count, following a three-day jury trial in Ashland County District Court. Though the defense of justification was disallowed during the trial, George was able to testify about the moral and legal basis for his action. The jury was also allowed to hear the testimony of Professor Francis Boyle on the application of international law to nuclear weapons policy and citizen responsibility. On February 12, 1988, George was sentenced to thirty-three months. In July 1988 he was denied parole. On May 2, 1989 his appeal was denied by the Wisconsin Court of Appeals and the court ruled his sabotage conviction valid.

AUSTRALIAN PLOWSHARES ACTION. On December 28, 1987, the feast of the Holy Innocents, Marie Grunke, a Blessed Sacrament Sister of Newtown, Joanne Merrigan and Anthony Gwyther, both of the St. Francis House, Darlinghurst, boarded the USS *Leftwich* during a public inspection while it was anchored in Sydney Harbor. The USS *Leftwich* is a nuclear-capable destroyer of the Spruance class recently deployed in the Persian Gulf. Recalling the innocents that were killed by King Herod and those children that continue to die from war and hunger, they poured their own blood on an ASROC anti-submarine nuclear depth charge launcher and a Tomahawk cruise missile launcher—weapons of first-strike capability. They hammered on these weapons to begin their disarmament and initiate their conversion into instruments of peace. After leaving their action statement on the ship, they were escorted off without being arrested or charged.

NUCLEAR NAVY PLOWSHARES. On Easter Sunday, April 3, 1988, Philip Berrigan of Jonah House (and original Plowshares Eight); Andrew Lawrence of the Community for Creative Nonviolence; Sister Margaret McKenna, a Doctor of Theology and member of the Medical Mission Sisters in Philadelphia; and Greg Boertje, former Army officer and member of Trident II Pruning Hooks and Epiphany Plowshares, boarded the battleship *Iowa* at Norfolk Naval Station in Virginia. The four boarded the battleship as part of a public tour greeting the vessel on its return from service in the Persian Gulf. The four disarmed two armored box launchers for the Tomahawk Cruise Missile, hammering and pouring blood, and unfurled two banners: SEEK THE DISARMED CHRIST, and TOMAHAWKS INTO PLOWSHARES.

The four worked for two or three minutes before they were seen by security. When ordered to stop they did so: a "security alert" was sounded and the pier was vacated of all but naval personnel. Hundreds of people had come on Easter Sunday to visit the USS *Iowa* and the USS *America* which was also on display. Tours of both vessels were shut down.

Andrew, Greg, Margaret, and Phil were held for some time at the naval base, questioned by the FBI and then transported by the FBI to Virginia Beach. They appeared in court on April 4, were charged with criminal trespass—a charge which does not entitle defendants to a jury trial—and all except Greg were held on $2,500 bond. Because of Greg's status as a fugitive (stemming from his non-appearance at the sentencing for the Epiphany Plowshares) he was held on $25,000 bond. They were tried before a U.S. Magistrate on May 19,1988, at the Norfolk Virginia Federal Court and convicted of trespass.

In an effort to diffuse courtroom support, the sentencing of the four was set on different days during July 1989. Margaret was sentenced to time served (over three months), two years probation and 240 hours community service, and prohibited from entering any military installation during her probation. She was then released. Andrew received a four-month sentence. Greg and Phil each received the maximum sentence of 6 months.

In March 1989 Margaret received a four-month jail sentence for refusing to cooperate with the conditions of her probation. However, she was credited with the time she already served before trial and ordered to jail for twenty days.

KAIROS PLOWSHARES. In the pre-dawn hours of June 26, 1988, Kathleen Maire, a Franciscan sister of Allegheny, N.Y.; Jack Marth, a member of POTS (Part of the Solution) in the Bronx, N.Y.; Sister Anne Montgomery, a participant in three previous Plowshares actions; and Christine Mulready, member of the Sisters of St. Joseph of Brentwood, N.Y., approached the Trident submarine USS *Pennsylvania* at EB in Groton, CT, with the intent of carrying out a symbolic act of disarmament. Paddling against the current in the midst of a fast approaching storm, they were spotted in their rubber rafts in the Thames River by EB security before reaching the Trident. Apprehended by EB security, they were held overnight in jail. They were arraigned on charges of trespass, conspiracy to commit criminal mischief, and criminal intent, and fined $40 for failure to use a light on their raft. They were released on a PTA and the charges were eventually dropped.

KAIROS PLOWSHARES TOO. On August 1, 1988, Kathleen Maire and Anne Montgomery, acting in the spirit of the four Kairos Plowshares, continued their Plowshares process by entering the EB facility in Quonset Point, R.I., where they hammered and poured blood on Trident submarine parts. They held a banner which read: "Trident D-5 Into Plowshares" and were quickly apprehended. They were charged with malicious mischief and trespass and then released on a PTA. On September 27th they were tried by a judge in South Kingston, R.I. In a trial that lasted only ninety minutes, they were convicted by the judge of the above charges. They were sentenced to six months supervised probation and ordered to pay $250 in restitution for the fence they cut. After Kathy and Anne told the judge that, for reasons of conscience, they wouldn't pay the restitution or cooperate with probation, he changed their probation to "unsupervised" and fined them $250. To date they have not paid the fine.

CREDO PLOWSHARES. On September 20, 1988, Marcia Timmel, of the Plowshares Four, mother and member of the Olive Branch Catholic Worker in Washington, D.C., entered the Sheraton-Washington hotel, site of the Air Force Association Arms Bazaar. Once inside she hammered and poured blood on a Textron Defense System (TDS) MX missile display, thereby dismantling it, and was subsequently arrested. She left at the site a statement decrying the blasphemous theme of the Arms Bazaar, "Freedom: A Creed To Believe In," and issued her own credo of life, faith, and love for the human family. During her two-day jury trial in D.C. Superior Court, she used promotional literature of TDS, producer of the MX, to demonstrate the clear intent of TDS and the Air Force to prevail on Congress for the deployment of fifty new MX missiles. "We've been making $200 million a year for the last 10 years on this," said a TDS employee. "She took that model down the first day of the exhibition and we couldn't use it. She probably deprived us of a chance to persuade a couple members of Congress."

Under the constraints of a jury instruction that relieved the government prosecution of the need to prove evil intent, the jury convicted Marcia on November 18, 1988, of property damage. On December 29, she was sentenced to ninety days, eighty-three days suspended pending completion of probation (ninety days), and ordered to serve seven days beginning January 9, 1989.

DUTCH DISARMAMENT ACTION. On December 8, 1988, the first anniversary of the INF Treaty, fourteen Dutch peace activists, calling themselves "INF Ploughshares," cut through fences to enter the Woensdrecht Airbase and made their way to cruise missile bunkers where they carried out the first disarmament action in Holland. In their action statement they declared: "The INF Treaty was signed to eliminate the ground-launched cruise and Pershing missiles from Europe. But the amount of air- and sea-launched missiles for European battlefield is increasing enormously and NATO plans are ready to modernize nuclear forces in Europe. The bunkers of cruise missiles won't be destroyed but given a new military destination. We oppose these new steps in the arms race. . . . We have started demolishing the cruise missile bunkers . . . by beating the bunker steel into ploughshares with sledgehammers. We demand that the money destined for new arms be spent instead on producing food for the hungry, detoxifying toxic waste dumps, and cleaning polluted water." They were subsequently apprehended and most were released by Dutch authorities after being held for thirty hours. Kees Koning was released after eight days.

NF-5B PLOWSHARES. On January 1, 1989, Kees Koning, an ex-army chaplain and priest, and Co van Melle, a medical doctor working with homeless people and illegal refugees, both of whom participated in the INF disarmament action, entered the Woensdrecht Airbase once again, and began the conversion of NF-5B fighter airplanes by beating them with sledgehammers into plowshares. The Dutch plan to sell the NF-5B to Turkey for use against the Kurdish nationalists, is part of a NATO aid program which involves shipping of sixty fighter planes to Turkey. They were charged with trespassing, sabotage, and $350,000 damage. They were detained in jail through their trial and received nationwide media attention. They were tried before three judges on February 9, 1989. Among those who were allowed to testify at the trial were a Kurdish lawyer, a former Dutch air force officer, and Phil Berrigan. They were sentenced to six months imprisonment but released pending appeal.

OTHER DUTCH DISARMAMENT ACTIONS

*On February 9, 1989*, Dutch activists Ad Hennen and Rolland van Hell, who were inspired by the two previous disarmament actions, entered a Dutch military base and started the conversion of Hawk missiles with axes. Ad was released pending trial but Roland continues to be detained because of his previous record.

*On Good Friday, March 24, 1989*, Kees Koning, who had participated in the first two Dutch disarmament actions, entered a Dutch airbase and with a pick axe began disarming a fighter plane destined for Turkey. He was subsequently arrested.

STOP WEAPONS EXPORTS—PLOWSHARES 2. On February 16, 1989 the first Plowshares action occurred in Sweden. Anders Grip, a truck driver who works with a group providing material aid to the Third World, and Gunilla Akerberg, a consultant for organic farming, entered a railroad yard in Kristinehamn where weapons waited to be shipped to an Indian boat on the west coast of Sweden. They damaged the loading mechanism of the Haubits 77B mobile anti-aircraft missile launcher with hammers. They then displayed a banner, saying: "Disarmament has begun," "We must dare to be disobedient," "Violence and oppression depend upon our obedience and passivity." When the police came a half-hour later, Anders and Gunilla had set up a dining table and invited the police to join them in a meal. They were placed under arrest. On their way to the police station, several of the police expressed support for their action and advised them of another potential site for a Plowshares action. They were released later that night. As of March 1989 charges had not yet been filed against them.

# *Appendix II*

## *Addresses of Plowshares Disarmament Support Groups*

Silo Pruning Hooks/Woodson
Family Support Group
Gaudete Peace and Justice
Center
634 Spruce St.
Madison, Wisconsin 53715
608-257-4996

Pershing Plowshares Support
Committee
P.O. Box 585
Orlando, FL 32802
305-830-1204

Witness for Peace at AVCO
Box 736
Wilmington, MA 01887
617-265-1236

Martin Holladay-Plowshares
Defense Fund
PO Box 61
Sheffield, VT 05866
802-626-8322

Silo Plowshares Support Group
1020 S. Wabash Ave., Rm 401
Chicago, IL 60605-2215
312-427-4351

Pershings To Plowshares
c/o Bill Boston
Forststr. 9
7000 Stuttgart 1
Germany
49-711-625-109

Jonah House
1933 Park Ave.
Baltimore, MD 21217
301-669-6265

Isaiah Peace Ministry
66 Edgewood Ave.
New Haven, CT 06511
203-562-7935

Plowshares N.Y.
2763 Webster Avenue
Bronx, NY 10458
212-220-4227

Epiphany Plowshare Support
    Group
Montgomery Co. Center for
    Peace & Justice
PO Box 246, Ambler, PA 19002
215-630-8540

Katya Komisaruk Defense
    Collective
1716 Felton St.
San Francisco, CA 94134
415-821-3346

Australian Plowshares Support
c/o Marie Grunke, 43 Forbes St.
Newtown, N.S.W. 2042
    Australia
(02) 516-1534

Transfiguration Plowshares West
    Support Group
635 E. 61st St.
Kansas City, MO 64110
816-361-1014

Harmonic Disarmament for Life
    Support Group
c/o Fr. Ed Beutner
Rt 3, Box 324
Ashland, WI 54806
715-746-2549

Dutch Plowshares Support Group
c/o H. Bosman sstr. 29
1077 XG Amsterdam
The Netherlands

Swedish Plowshares
c/o Per Herngren
Vasterslant 56
424 35 Angered
Sweden

# Appendix III

## Swords into Plowshares

In 1980, the arms race, "a machine gone mad" in the words of the Vatican Declaration of 1976, was seen by many as inevitable, beyond challenge. Most people avoided thinking about it or accepted the endless production of weapons as a necessary evil, part of the system of deterrence, meant to prevent nuclear war.

Yet planning and production of a system capable of launching a nuclear first strike was well along. This was described as "maintaining the credibility of deterrence." In other words, the U.S. was trying convincingly to demonstrate our intention actually to use these weapons, to "prevail" in a nuclear war; even if it meant putting nuclear war on hair trigger or launching a "preemptive" strike.

In taking to heart the words of the prophets Isaiah and Micah, we determined to "beat swords into plowshares." On September 9, 1980 we walked into a General Electric plant in King of Prussia, Pennsylvania and took hammers to two warheads for Mark 12A Minuteman III missiles. We saw our action as one of hope for the future and gratitude for God's creation which was—and is—under threat of planetary extinction.

We wanted our action to ring with the truth that everyone can take responsibility for the weapons produced in our name. Our act was, simply, a response to the Gospel injunction to love our enemies.

During our trial we attempted to say that it is illegal under international law to build these weapons and that we had acted in accord with the Nuremberg precept that citizens must act to prevent crimes against humanity. To prepare for nuclear war is to prepare for genocide and ecocide.

Since 1980, millions of people have found ways nonviolently to challenge the lie that weapons provide security. Tens of thousands of people have been civilly disobedient; some of these are now serving prison sentences ranging up to eighteen years for plowshares actions.

Nonviolent movements around the world challenge the rule of violence—in South Africa, in Poland, East Germany and China, in Latin America and the Middle East. Opposition to nuclear weapons has sprung up everywhere—from the Pacific rim to Europe to every weapons installation in the U.S.

Nuclear winter studies have made clear the threat that nuclear war poses to the entire planet. Revelations of the environmental devastation caused by the production of nuclear bombs gives new impetus to the demand to halt all such production.

The Soviet Union has taken astonishing initiatives for disarmament and has begun to dismantle Cold War structures. No longer a distant dream, the path toward a future based on ideas of common security is before us. In many ways, everything has changed.

But has it? Today tens of billions of desperately needed dollars are still squandered on wasteful and dangerous weapons systems. The poor, specially the children, continue to be victimized by General Electric's and other corporations' larcenous hold on the public treasury. Both the rate of poverty and the military budget were doubled during the 1980s.

In 1980, GE received $3 million a day in military contracts. By 1987, the total reached over $15 million a day for GE alone, a corporation found guilty of defrauding the government of $800,000 when they falsified claims for Mark 12A production.

Today we return to court for re-sentencing after nine years of appealing to the courts to act as protector of the life of the community. We also return to General Electric to say, THE CRIME IS HERE.

Daniel Berrigan, SJ
Philip Berrigan
Dean Hammer
Carl Kabat, OMI

Elmer Maas
Anne Montgomery, RCSJ
Molly Rush
John Schurchardt
"The Plowshares Eight"
1989

# Bibliography

Appleton, Sarah Weber, ed., GRIFFISS PLOWSHARES ACTION AND TRIAL: Trial Sequence, Notes and Texts of Testimonies, Comment and News Coverage. Syracuse: Plowshares Support, 1984.

Behrens, Laurence and Leonard J. *Writing and Reading Across the Curriculum* (second ed.) Boston: Little, Brown, 1985.

Berrigan, Daniel. *Night Flight To Hanoi.* New York: Harper & Row, 1968.

———— *Portraits of Those I Love.* New York: Crossroad, 1984.

———— *Steadfastness of the Saints.* Maryknoll: Orbis Books, 1985.

———— *To Dwell in Peace.* New York: Harper & Row, 1987.

———— *The Trial of the Catonsville Nine.* Boston: Beacon Press, 1970.

Berrigan, Philip. *Prison Journals of a Priest Revolutionary.* New York: Ballantine, 1967.

———— *Widen the Prison Gates.* New York: Simon & Schuster, 1973.

Berrigan, Philip, and Elizabeth McAlister. *The Time's Discipline: The Beatitudes and Nuclear Resistance.* Baltimore: Fortkamp Publishing Co., 1989.

Bok, Sissela. *A Strategy For Peace: Human Values and the Threat of War.* New York: Pantheon, 1989.

Bonhoeffer, Dietrich, *Letters and Papers From Prison.* New York: Macmillan, 1953.

Boyer, Richard O. and Herbert M. Morais. *Labor's Untold Story.* New York: United Electrical, Radio and Machine Workers of America, 1955.

Caldicott, Helen. *Nuclear Madness. What You can Do!* Brookline, Mass.: Autumn Press, 1978.

Caulfield, Catherine. *Multiple Exposures.* New York: Harper & Row, 1989.

Coles, Robert. *Dorothy Day: A Radical Devotion.* Reading, Mass.: Addison-Wesley, 1987.

———. *Simone Weil, A Modern Pilgrimage.* Reading, Mass.: Addison-Wesley, 1986.

Del Tredici, Robert. *At Work in the Fields of the Bomb.* New York: Harper & Row, 1987.

Eaton, Jeanette. *Gandhi: Fighter Without a Sword.* New York: William Morrow, 1950.

Ford, Daniel. *Cult of the Atom: The Secret Papers of the Atomic Energy Commission.* New York: Simon & Schuster, 1982.

Ford, Daniel, Henry Kendall, and Steven Nadis. *Beyond the Freeze: The Road to Nuclear Sanity.* Boston: Beacon Press, 1982.

Fradkin, Philip L. *Fallout: An American Nuclear Tragedy.* Tucson: The University of Arizona Press, 1989.

Fuller, John G. *We Almost Lost Detroit.* New York: Reader's Digest Press, 1975.

Gofman, John W. *"Irrevy": An Irreverent, Illustrated View of Nuclear Power.* San Francisco: Committee for Nuclear Responsibility, 1979.

Gofman, John W. and Arthur R. Tamplin. *Poisoned Power: The Case Against Nuclear Power Plants.* Emmaus: Rodale Press, 1971.

Gray, Francine du Plessix. *Divine Disobedience.* New York: Vintage, 1969.

Groueff, Stephane. *Manhattan Project: The Untold Story of the Making of the Atomic Bomb.* Boston: Little, Brown, 1967.

Gyorgy, Anna, and friends. *No Nukes: Everyone's Guide to Nuclear Power.* Boston: South End Press, 1979.

Hemingway, Ernest. *In Our Time.* New York: Scribners, 1925.

Hersey, John. *Hiroshima.* New York: Knopf, 1946.

Japan Broadcasting Corporation, ed. *Unforgettable Fire.* New York: Pantheon, 1977.

Jung, Robert. *The New Tyranny: How Nuclear Power Enslaves Us.* New York: Grosset & Dunlap, 1979.

Kennan, George F. *The Nuclear Delusion: Soviet-American Relations in the Atomic Age.* New York: Pantheon, 1976.

Kirschner, Allen and Linda, eds. *Blessed are the Peacemakers*. New York: Popular Library, 1971.

Laffin, Arthur J., and Anne Montgomery, eds. *Swords into Plowshares: Nonviolent Direct Action For Disarmament*. New York: Harper & Row, 1986.

Lens, Sidney. *Radicalism in America*. New York: Crowell, 1969.

Lifton, Robert Jay, and Richard Falk. *Indefensible Weapons*. New York: Basic Books, 1982.

Litz, Walton A., ed. *Major American Short Stories*. New York: Oxford, 1980.

Merton, Thomas. *Raids On The Unspeakable*. New York: New Directions, 1964.

————. *The Nonviolent Alternative*. New York: Farrar, Straus, 1971.

Miranda, Jose. *Marx and the Bible: A Critique of the Philosophy of Oppression*. Maryknoll: Orbis Books, 1971.

————. *Communism In the Bible*. Maryknoll: Orbis Books, 1985.

Mojtabai, A. G. *Blessed Assurance: At Home with the Bomb In Amarillo, Texas*. Boston: Houghton Mifflin, 1986.

Mott, Michael. *The Seven Mountains of Thomas Merton*. Boston: Houghton Mifflin, 1984.

Novick, Sheldon. *The Careless Atom*. Boston: Houghton Mifflin, 1969.

Rosenthal, Debra. *At the Heart of the Bomb: The Dangerous Allure of Weapons Work*. Reading, Mass.: Addison-Wesley, 1990.

Scholl, Inge. *The White Rose: Munich 1942–1943*. Middletown: Wesleyan, 1970.

Stephenson, Lee, and George R. Zachar, eds. *Accidents Will Happen: The Case Against Nuclear Power*. New York: Harper & Row, 1979.

*Shutdown: Nuclear Power On Trial*. Summertown: The Book Publishing Company, 1979.

Thompson, E. P., and Dan Smith, eds. *Protest and Survive*. New York: Monthly Review Press, 1981.

Totten, Sam, and Martha Wescoat Totten. *Facing The Danger*. Trumansburg: The Crossing Press, 1984.

Tourner, Paul. *The Violence Within*. New York: Harper & Row, 1977.

Wallis, Jim. *Waging Peace: A Handbook for the Struggle to Abolish Nuclear Weapons*. New York: Harper & Row, 1982.

Wasserman, Harvey. *Energy War: Reports from the Front.* Westport, Conn.: Lawrence Hill, 1979.

Zinn, Howard. *The Twentieth Century: A People's History,* New York: Harper & Row, 1984.

Zuckerman, Solly. *Nuclear Illusion and Reality.* New York: Vintage, 1982.

# Index